Legged Alarm Clocks

Dennis H. Sagvold

Schiffer Publishing Ltd

4880 Lower Valley Road, Atglen, PA 19310 USA

Dedication

DEDICATED TO MY THREE LOVELY DAUGHTERS
De Von
Renee
Melissa
AND THEIR FAMILIES

Title page: Author's collection.

Library of Congress Control Number: 2003113692

Designed by Joseph M. Riggio Jr.
Type set in Americana XBd BT/Humanist 521 BT

ISBN: 0-7643-1997-3
Printed in China

Published by Schiffer Publishing Ltd.
4880 Lower Valley Road
Atglen, PA 19310
Phone: (610) 593-1777; Fax: (610) 593-2002
E-mail: Info@schifferbooks.com

In Europe, Schiffer books are distributed by
Bushwood Books
6 Marksbury Ave.
Kew Gardens
Surrey TW9 4JF England
Phone: 44 (0) 20 8392-8585; Fax: 44 (0) 20 8392-9876
E-mail: info@bushwoodbooks.co.uk
Free postage in the U.K., Europe; air mail at cost.

Contents

Introduction

As early as the eighth century, clocks were invented to sound a controlled alarm. These were not clocks as we know them today. The first such was a Chinese fire alarm. There was a single incense stick over which several strings with balls were suspended. As the incense burned, it burned through each string, one at a time, and each string and ball would fall into a dish to sound an alarm.

With the invention of the clock spring, around 1450, and the invention of the verge and balance wheel around 1500, we had our first portable watch. For the first time we had the time wherever we went.

This book focuses on approximately a half century of early alarm clocks, as we know them today—a very important time in horological history. These alarms are known as "tin can alarms," or "nickel alarms." The early ones indeed *looked* as if they were made from tin cans. They were nickel-plated until later years when they took on other finishes, including painted finishes.

I refer to alarm clocks from this period as legged alarms, which covers all types as long as they have legs. Legged alarms were made in countless numbers by most clock manufacturers, starting around 1880, and gave way to the more modern solid base clocks around 1935.

Although legged alarms were *made* in countless numbers, very few *exist* today—probably because some of these clocks sold for as little as 49 cents; when they quit running they were not worth repairing and therefore were thrown away. On the other hand, who wanted a legged alarm when the new, modern-

A commemorative of the Spanish American War of 1898. Clock manufactured by Westclox, Pat. June 4, 1907. The dial has a patent date of 9-12-99 by Regent Mfg. Co., Chicago. The case is 6-1/4" tall with a 3-1/2" multi-colored dial. Brass legs and ring trim out the case. Alarm set is on back of case. The portraits are of President McKinley and the heroes of the Spanish American War. Clockwise they are: Schlev, Sampson, Sigsbee, Evans, Clark, Funston, Wheeler, Otis, Shafter, Roosevelt (Assistant Secretary of the Navy), Miles, and Commodore Dewey. *Photo by Linda Johnson.*

styled clocks with a base were available?! When you consider the many styles and improvements the alarm clock has gone through, you begin to realize why so few legged alarms exist today.

Styles changed on legged alarms. You will find bells on top of the case and also mounted on the back of the case. Brass cases are not common. You see some legged alarms with brass trim on the legs and top ornaments. Piecrust bezels are very hard to find. Calendar alarms are about impossible to locate. Striking alarms that strike the hour and half hour are very rare. Luminous dials are much harder to locate than white dials.

Among the rarities I enjoy are the private label dials. A retailer could have his name put on the dial of a clock at no additional charge if he ordered a required number of clocks. I believe the minimum order was one case. I have found more private label dials on Big Ben clocks than any other alarm. Not only does this make the clock scarcer, but it also reveals a very important part of history. The private label tells when a jeweler was in business and where he was located.

The values in this book are for excellent condition, restored clocks. Condition of the cases and dials are very important. A dark dial usually means the clock has been over-oiled and the oil seeped onto the dial. It cannot be brought back to original condition.

Clocks not in running condition and needing complete restoration would probably not be worth more than $15 or $20.

Legged alarms are not easy to find anymore. After all, the last ones were manufactured in the late 1930s. I believe legged alarms are by far underrated.

My prices have been based on clocks seen in antique shops, other price guides, and E-Bay.

Whether you are new to the collecting or have been at it for years, membership in a collector's club is a wonderful way to learn more and meet like-minded people. I recommend membership in:

The National Association of Watch and Clock Collectors (N.A.W.C.C.)
514 Poplar Street
Columbia, PA 17512-2130

Index by Manufacturer

Index by Model

American Manufacturers

Ansonia

The Ansonia Clock Company was located in Ansonia, Connecticut, between 1851 and 1878. Mr. Anson G. Phelps started the company in 1851 as a subsidiary of the Ansonia Brass Co. This became a very successful company and was a separate company in 1859, and incorporated in 1873.

In 1878 the company moved to New York and a year later, in 1879, was heavily damaged with fire. They resumed business in 1880.

Ansonia Clock Co. was a very successful company until 1930 when they sold everything, including their machinery, to Russia.

Amazon. The Ansonia Clock Co. 8-3/4" nickel case; 4-7/8" white dial. Seconds bit. Strikes hour and half hours. Value: $225

Bee, shown with original tin. 3" tall; 1-3/4" dial. Brass legs and ring, back wind. "BEE" stamped on bottom of case. Pat'd April 23, 1878. Value: $250

Buzzer Repeating. 6-1/4" tall; 3-1/4" white dial. Brass ring and legs, alarm shut off lever. Value: $125

No. 5L2923 Buzzer Repeating Alarm Clock, runs for 30 hours with one winding, made by the Ansonia Clock Co. This clock has all the advantages of a repeating alarm clock that sells from $1.25 to $1.50. It alarms at intervals of 5 seconds, stands 6½ inches high, dial is 4 inches in diameter.
Price.......... **89c**

If by mail, postage extra, 32 cents.

Campbell Electric Co., Lynn, Mass. 5-1/4" tall; 3-3/8" white dial. Top piece appears not original. Value: $95

The Commuter. 7-1/8" tall; 4" white dial. Alarm shut off top left, long intermittent top right. Value: $95

Clatter. 6-1/4" tall; 4" white dial. 1-26-14 scratched on case, possible repair date. Value: $115

Luminous. 6" tall; 3-1/4" dial. Brass legs. It appears that the entire dial was luminous. Value: $125

The National Call 8 Day Alarm. 6-1/2" tall; 4" white dial. 24-hour alarm set. Patents Feb. 24, 1914 through Nov. 10, 1914. Value: $100

Nestor. 6-1/4" tall; 3-1/4" dial. Brass legs and ring, brass winding knobs. Value: $125

Repeater. 7" tall; 3-7/8" white dial. Brass ring and legs, and alarm shut off lever. Pat'd Aug. 2, 1898. Value: $125

Simplex Eight Day. (Red letters). Time Alarm, Automatic. 6-1/8" tall; 4" white dial. 24-hour alarm set indicator. Pat'd Feb. 24, 1914 through Nov. 10, 1914. 5/18/15 scratched on case. Value: $125

Startler. M.W. Trade Mark (Montgomery Ward). 6-1/8" tall; 4" white dial. Pat'd Feb. 24, 1914 through Nov. 10, 1914. Value: $125

Trump, Intermittent. 5-1/2" tall; 3-1/2" dial. Shut off knob upper left. Value: $100

Pat'd March 27, 1877. Ansonia Trade Mark. 6-1/4" tall; 3-1/4" white dial. Brass ring and leg, one stove bolt leg, not original. Value: $125

Ansonia Trade Mark. 6-1/4" tall; 3-1/4" white dial. Brass ring and legs. Value: $125

Patent appl'd for Ansonia Trade Mark. 5-1/2" tall; 3-1/4" white dial. Second bit, brass ring and legs, time only. Value: $95

Ansonia. 3-1/2" tall; 2-1/4" dial. Shut off upper right, large hand is alarm set. Value: $90

Pat'd April 23, 1878. 3-1/4" tall; 1-11/16" white dial. Back wind, brass ring, and legs. Time only. Value: $95

Ansonia Trade Mark. 3-1/4" tall; 1-13/16" white dial. Second bit, time only. Pat'd May 3, 1892. Value: $90

Manufactured by Ansonia Clock Co. There is some type of timing device on the back of the clock. A brass piece with 5 spiral grooves is located on the hand set shaft. When the arm is placed on a groove of any choice, it moves toward the end of spiral and falls down. 5-1/2" tall; 3-1/4" white dial. Second bit, time only, brass ring and legs. Value: $150

Ansonia trade mark. 3-3/8" tall; 1-3/4" white dial. Brass ring, time only. Value: $90

Ansonia Clock Co. C.D. Taylor, Jeweler. 311 Front St. Mankato, Minn. 3-1/4" paper dial; 6-1/4" nickel-plated case, with brass top piece. Scratched on back "Nov 9, 1899-$2.00" Value: $175

Attleboro

There is very little known about the Attleboro Clock Co. The few clocks I have inspected have other manufacturers movements. It appears that Attleboro Clock Co. used other companies' movements, or entire clocks, and put their name on them.

Attleboro Clock Co., Attleboro, Mass. 5-5/16" tall; 3-1/4" white dial. Scratched on back: 1897 Okt. 15th, $7.00. Seems like a lot of money in 1897. Value: $150

Gilbert

The Gilbert Clock Company has a long history of many partners, in several locations in Connecticut. Gilbert Clocks started in 1806 with several different partners and name changes that all included the Gilbert name.

They became Wm. L. Gilbert from 1850 to 1866, in 1871 the Gilbert Manufacturing Co., and operated as William L. Gilbert Clock Co. until 1934, at which time it became the William L. Gilbert Clock Corp. In 1964 the company was sold to Spartus Clock Co. of Chicago, Illinois.

GILBERT

"Bell Hop"

The newest thing in clocks, combining beauty with utility. A household innovation, colorful and charming in appearance, and withal, precisely accurate. The Bell Hop is an indefatigable servant, always on the job always prompt, always trustworthy. It will time the cooking, announce the baby's feeding time as well as arousing the family in the morning. A wall bracket is furnished with each clock—for the first time establishing a secure resting place for the kitchen clock. Made in six attractive colors—Gray, Rose, Blue, Cream, Green, Lavendar. 40 hour intermittent alarm feature.

No. 4609—Diameter, 4 ½ inches. Each.........$3.25

Packed in cartons of 24; shipping weight 42 lbs.

Clock your Home with Gilberts
ASK your dealer to show you these dual purpose clocks with the exclusively Gilbert radium dials. They are the answer to your quest for a clock that will tell the time distinctly and unmistakably in the dark of the night.
The clear visibility of Gilbert radium dials is a unique Gilbert achievement attained through concentrating radium upon the hands and upon the compact markings placed inside of numerals. This means intensified radiance where light is wanted—instead of a blurred circle of diffused light resulting from radium spread thinly all over hands and numerals.
The effectiveness of the radium is guaranteed for at least five years.
DEALERS:—Handle Gilberts—the perfected Radium Clocks. Your customers are relying on your progressiveness. Write for paying proposition
GILBERT
Night and Day
Radium Dial Clocks
WILLIAM L. GILBERT CLOCK COMPANY
Dept. L. D.
Makers of Good Clocks Since 1807 at
Winsted Connecticut
WINLITE—RADIUM DIAL
Intermittent alarm. One day movement. 6¾ inches high.
No. 1143—GRACEFUL
Mahogany. Hand rubbed finish. 20½ inches wide, 9¾ inches high.
GILBERT NINE—RADIUM DIAL
Nine day clock with automatic alarm. 7 inches high.

Long Range Visibility For Your Comfort
Clearly readable across the room, the time of night glows from the strongly luminous markings of
GILBERT Night and Day
Radium Dial Clocks
An extraordinary convenience in the bedroom, in the sick-room, in every room of the house.
Long experimenting has proved the better and clearer visibility of these capable clocks. Only Radium Gilberts "make night time plain as day."
Accuracy, beauty and utility are combined in these perfected timepieces.
WILLIAM L. GILBERT CLOCK CO.
DEPT. S
Makers of good clocks since 1807 at
WINSTED CONNECTICUT
You'll find among the several fascinating models just the one you need. Ask your dealer to supply you.
Dealers: Supply Gilbert Radium Clocks, the clocks of longer and stronger night visibility. Write for proposition.
WINLITE—RADIUM DIAL
Intermittent alarm—one day movement, 6¾ inches high
MOONLITE—RADIUM DIAL
Has a one day time movement, in polished mahogany case, 5 inches high, with 3 inch dial
GILBERT NINE—RADIUM DIAL
Nine day clock with automatic alarm, 7 inches high

G.C.Co. (Manufactured by Gilbert Clock Co.) 3-3/4" paper dial; 6-1/2" nickel-plated case, with brass legs and top piece. Scratched on the back "cleaned Oct 3, 1893". This is the earliest trade mark I have seen on a Gilbert clock. Value: $150

Barrage. 5-3/4" tall; 4" white dial. Alarm shut off on back. Value: $90

Bell Hop. 6" tall; 4" silver paper dial with luminous numerals. Convex glass, brass case (once painted). Pat'd June 6, 1922. Value: $75

Connecticut, intermittent. 6-3/4" tall; 4-1/4" white dial. Convex glass, alarm shut off, upper left. Pat'd June 6, 1922. Value: $90

Design. 5-3/4" tall; 3-7/8" white dial. Shut off upper left. Pat'd June 6, 1922. Value: $90

Intermittent, Private label dial. W.H. Broer 427 Summit St., Toledo, Ohio. 6" tall; 3-3/4" white dial. Alarm shut off on top behind top piece, lever on back for choice of continuous or intermittent alarm. Pat'd Jan. 25, 98 through Jan. 19, 09. Value: $175

Nine. 6-7/8" tall; 4" white dial. 24-hour alarm set, shut off on top and behind ring, repeat knob in center of ring. Second bit. Value: $115

Tornado. (Manufactured by Gilbert Clock Co.) 4" silver paper dial with white and black numerals. 6-3/4" nickel-plated case. Value: $125

Tornado. 6-1/4" tall; 4" white dial. Shut off on back left. 12-14 scratched on back (repair date?) Value: $125

Twilite. 6-1/2" tall; 4" dial. Luminous markers and hands, light blue time track. Value: $125

U.S. 3-1/2" tall; 2-3/8" dial. Seconds bit, time only. Made for the Air Corps Military Medical. Value: $95

Winlite intermittent. 6-3/4" tall; 4" dial. Luminous markers and hands, light blue time track, alarm shut off on top behind ring. Value: $110

Private label dial. M'F'D' expressly for Edwin Pape, Jeweler, Davenport, Iowa. Manufactured by Gilbert Clock Co. 6-1/4" tall; 3-3/8" dial. Brass ring and legs. Pat'd Jan. 25, 1898. 12-27-02 scratched on back. Value: $175

Gilbert. 6" tall; 4" white dial. Pat'd June 6, 1922. Value: $90

Ingersoll

In 1892, Robert H. Ingersoll and his brother started the Ingersoll Company in Waterbury, Connecticut. They developed a huge business of inexpensive watches, producing 40,000 the first year.

In 1908 they bought the Trenton Watch Co. Later they had a large contract with Waterbury Clock Co. for dollar watches.

Waterbury bought the Ingersoll Company in 1922.

Petite. 3-3/8" black painted and nickel case; 2-1/4" white dial. Shut off on top of case, Convex glass. Value: $75

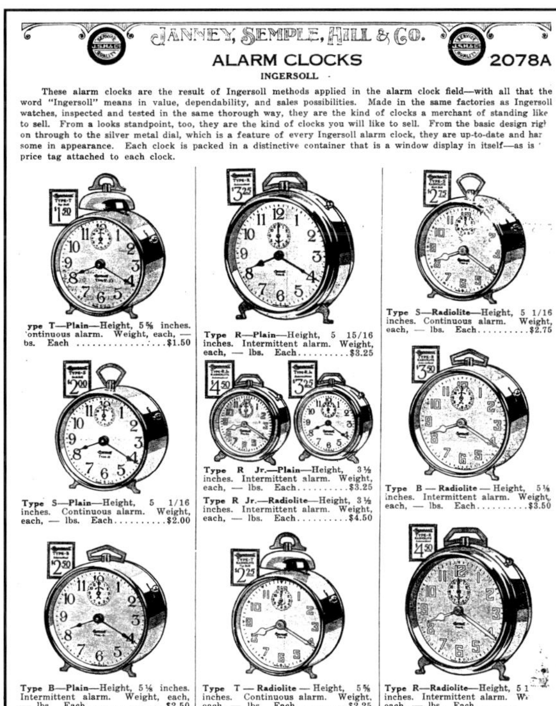

JANNEY, SEMPLE, HILL & CO.

ALARM CLOCKS — 2078A

INGERSOLL

These alarm clocks are the result of Ingersoll methods applied in the alarm clock field—with all that the word "Ingersoll" means in value, dependability, and sales possibilities. Made in the same factories as Ingersoll watches, inspected and tested in the same thorough way, they are the kind of clocks a merchant of standing like to sell. From a looks standpoint, too, they are the kind of clocks you will like to sell. From the basic design rig on through to the silver metal dial, which is a feature of every Ingersoll alarm clock, they are up-to-date and har some in appearance. Each clock is packed in a distinctive container that is a window display in itself—as is price tag attached to each clock.

Type T—Plain—Height, 5⅝ inches. Continuous alarm. Weight, each, — lbs. Each $1.50

Type R—Plain—Height, 5 15/16 inches. Intermittent alarm. Weight, each, — lbs. Each..........$3.25

Type S—Radiolite—Height, 5 1/16 inches. Continuous alarm. Weight, each, — lbs. Each..........$2.75

Type S—Plain—Height, 5 1/16 inches. Continuous alarm. Weight, each, — lbs. Each..........$2.00

Type R Jr.—Plain—Height, 3½ inches. Intermittent alarm. Weight, each, — lbs. Each..........$3.25

Type R Jr.—Radiolite—Height, 3½ inches. Intermittent alarm. Weight, each, — lbs. Each..........$4.50

Type B—Radiolite—Height, 5⅛ inches. Intermittent alarm. Weight, each, — lbs. Each..........$3.50

Type B—Plain—Height, 5⅛ inches. Intermittent alarm. Weight, each, — lbs. Each................$2.50

Type T—Radiolite—Height, 5⅝ inches. Continuous alarm. Weight, each, — lbs. Each..........$2.25

Type R—Radiolite—Height, 5 1 inches. Intermittent alarm. Wt each, — lbs. Each........

Type B. 5" tall; 3-5/8" silver metal dial. Shut off lever located on the top right. Shown with original box. Value: $175

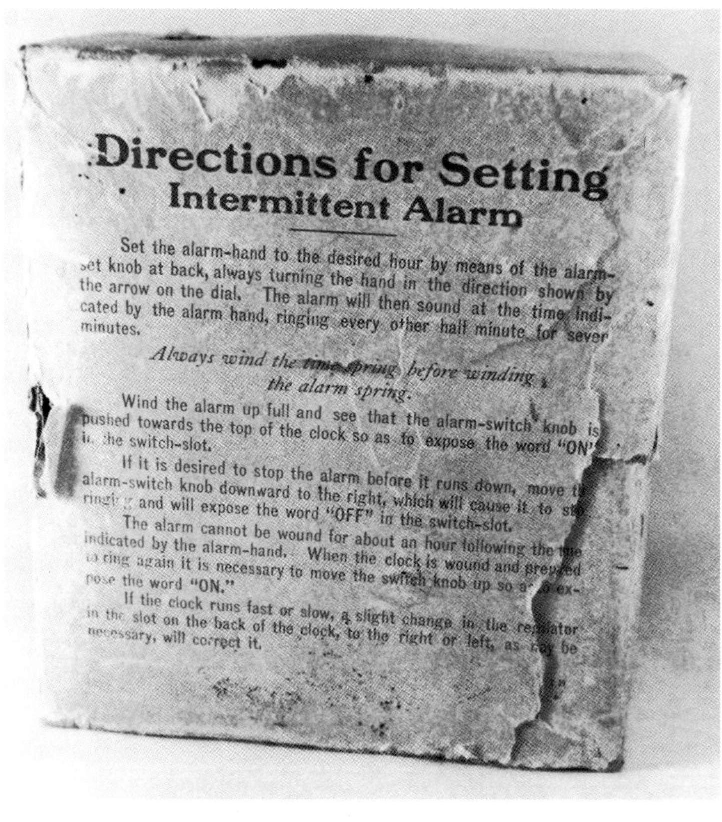

Original box. 5-1/4" wide; 6" high; 4" deep. Off white cardboard with green ink. Bottom of box shows complete instructions.

Type R. 6" green painted case; 4" silver metal dial. Nickel top, legs, and shut off knob. Pat'd Jan. 29, 1918 to Jan. 2, 1923. Value: $110

Type R. 6" black painted case; 4" silver metal dial. Nickel top, legs, and shut off knob. Different style numerals. Value: $110

NOVEMBER, 1927 21

Ingersoll
announces–
ALARM CLOCKS

And now . . .

INGERSOLL ALARM CLOCKS—made by the makers of Ingersoll Watches—with all that the name Ingersoll means in quality, reliability, style and value.

You'll respect the way these Ingersoll clocks keep time; you'll admire their looks. Basically of tasteful design and proportions they have many features that will appeal to you: metal dials—heavy rolled edge cases—artistic hands and numerals—handles and feet that are part of the clock rather than merely attachments—knob alarm switches.

Five models, each in plain dial or luminous—priced from $1.50 to $4.50. You'll find them on sale at Ingersoll dealers' everywhere. If your dealer has not yet stocked them, write us mentioning his name.

Five Models, "Plain" or "Luminous" to Choose from

Type-T	$1.50	Type-T Radiolite	$2.25
Type-S	2.00	Type-S Radiolite	2.75
Type-B	2.50	Type-B Radiolite	3.50
Type-R	3.25	Type-R Radiolite	4.50
Type-R Jr.	3.25	Type-R Jr. Radiolite	4.50

INGERSOLL WATCH CO., Inc.

Type R. Jr. 3-1/2" tall; 2-1/8" silver metal dial. Pat'd June 4, 1907 to Jan. 29, 1918. Value: $95

Type S. 5" tall; 3-3/8" silver metal dial. Pat'd Jan. 29, 1918. Value: $100

Type T. 5-5/8" tall; 3-3/8" silver metal dial. Pat'd Nov. 29, 1910 to June 7, 1921. Value: $125

Type T. 6-1/4" tall; 3-3/8" silver metal dial. Luminous numerals. Pat'd Dec. 15, 1908, Mfg'd 12-17-1924. Value: $125

Ingraham

Elias Ingraham founded his clock business in 1831 and ran it until 1843. At that time, he went with Brewster Manufacturing Co., which became Brewster and Ingraham from 1844 to 1852.

From 1852 to 1856, the firm was known as E. & A.. Ingraham (for Elias and Andrew Ingraham) .

The company was known as E. & A. Ingraham & Co. from 1856 to 1857; Elias Ingraham & Co. from 1857 to 1861; E Ingraham & Co. from 1861 to 1880; the E. Ingraham & Co. from 1880 to 1884; and finally The Ingraham Co. from 1884 to 1958.

Ace (in red diamond). 6" tall; 3-1/4" white dial. Shut off inside ring. Value: $150

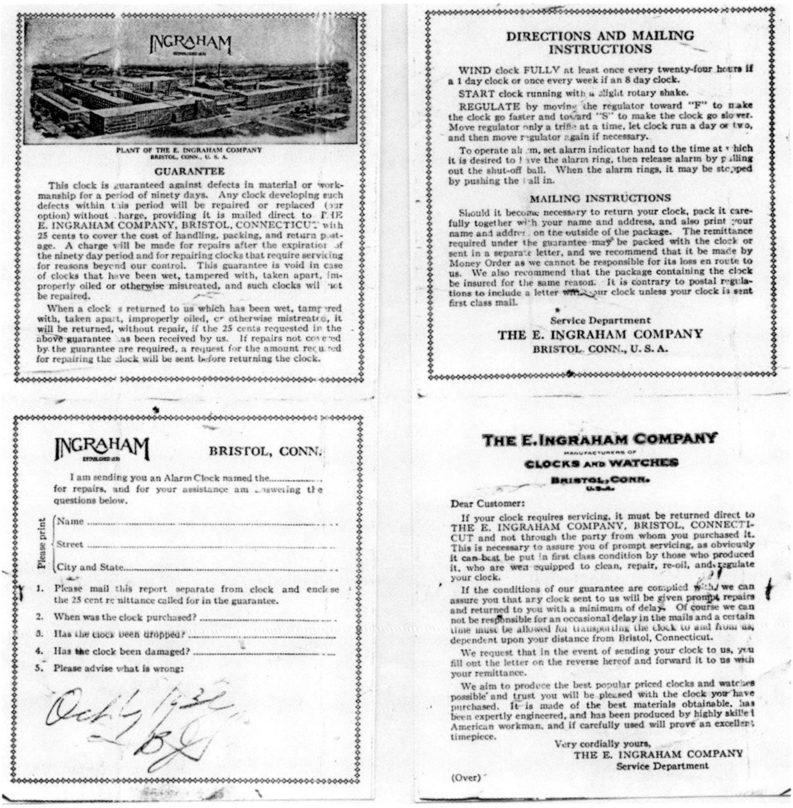

INGRAHAM

PLANT OF THE E. INGRAHAM COMPANY
BRISTOL, CONN., U. S. A.

GUARANTEE

This clock is guaranteed against defects in material or workmanship for a period of ninety days. Any clock developing such defects within this period will be repaired or replaced (our option) without charge, providing it is mailed direct to THE E. INGRAHAM COMPANY, BRISTOL, CONNECTICUT with 25 cents to cover the cost of handling, packing, and return postage. A charge will be made for repairs after the expiration of the ninety day period and for repairing clocks that require servicing for reasons beyond our control. This guarantee is void in case of clocks that have been wet, tampered with, taken apart, improperly oiled or otherwise mistreated, and such clocks will not be repaired.

When a clock is returned to us which has been wet, tampered with, taken apart, improperly oiled, or otherwise mistreated, it will be returned, without repair, if the 25 cents requested in the above guarantee has been received by us. If repairs not covered by the guarantee are required, a request for the amount required for repairing the clock will be sent before returning the clock.

DIRECTIONS AND MAILING INSTRUCTIONS

WIND clock FULLY at least once every twenty-four hours if a 1 day clock or once every week if an 8 day clock.

START clock running with a slight rotary shake.

REGULATE by moving the regulator toward "F" to make the clock go faster and toward "S" to make the clock go slower. Move regulator only a trifle at a time, let clock run a day or two, and then move regulator again if necessary.

To operate alarm, set alarm indicator hand to the time at which it is desired to have the alarm ring, then release alarm by pulling out the shut-off ball. When the alarm rings, it may be stopped by pushing the ball in.

MAILING INSTRUCTIONS

Should it become necessary to return your clock, pack it carefully together with your name and address, and also print your name and address on the outside of the package. The remittance required under the guarantee may be packed with the clock or sent in a separate letter, and we recommend that it be made by Money Order as we cannot be responsible for its loss en route to us. We also recommend that the package containing the clock be insured for the same reason. It is contrary to postal regulations to include a letter with your clock unless your clock is sent first class mail.

Service Department
THE E. INGRAHAM COMPANY
BRISTOL, CONN., U. S. A.

INGRAHAM BRISTOL, CONN.

I am sending you an Alarm Clock named the.................. for repairs, and for your assistance am answering the questions below.

Please print
Name ....
Street ....
City and State..

1. Please mail this report separate from clock and enclose the 25 cent remittance called for in the guarantee.
2. When was the clock purchased? ....
3. Has the clock been dropped? ....
4. Has the clock been damaged? ....
5. Please advise what is wrong:

THE E. INGRAHAM COMPANY
MANUFACTURERS OF
CLOCKS AND WATCHES
BRISTOL, CONN.
U.S.A.

Dear Customer:

If your clock requires servicing, it must be returned direct to THE E. INGRAHAM COMPANY, BRISTOL, CONNECTICUT and not through the party from whom you purchased it. This is necessary to assure you of prompt servicing, as obviously it can best be put in first class condition by those who produced it, who are well equipped to clean, repair, re-oil, and regulate your clock.

If the conditions of our guarantee are complied with, we can assure you that any clock sent to us will be given prompt repairs and returned to you with a minimum of delay. Of course we can not be responsible for an occasional delay in the mails and a certain time must be allowed for transporting the clock to and from us, dependent upon your distance from Bristol, Connecticut.

We request that in the event of sending your clock to us, you fill out the letter on the reverse hereof and forward it to us with your remittance.

We aim to produce the best popular priced clocks and watches possible and trust you will be pleased with the clock you have purchased. It is made of the best materials obtainable, has been expertly engineered, and has been produced by highly skilled American workman, and if carefully used will prove an excellent timepiece.

Very cordially yours,
THE E. INGRAHAM COMPANY
Service Department

(Over)

All Star Eight Day. 5-1/8" black painted case; 4" white and blue dial. Shut off on top. Value: $75

Ambassador. 5" tall; 3-3/8" white dial. Shut off knob in ring. Pat'd Dec. 3, 1912 to Jan. 14, 1913. Value: $95

Ambassador. 5-1/8" blue painted case; 3-3/8" blue paper dial. Nickel ring and legs. Value: $95

Break O' Day, long arm. 7" tall; 4-3/8" white dial. Shut off in ring, single ball leg in front, 2 legs on back. Pat'd Sep. 11, 1906 through Feb. 4, 1908. Value: $110

Break O' Day, intermittent. 6" tall; 3-1/4" white dial. Pat'd Sept. 11, 1906 through Dec. 10, 1912. Value: $95

Buffalo Dental Manufacturing Co. Buffalo, N.Y. U.S.A. (Manufactured by Ingraham Clock Co.) 3-1/4" paper dial; 5" black painted case. Must have been used to shut off a gas supply. The lever was set on which ever groove you chose. Each groove is one hour. The lever is spring loaded and when it comes to the end, drops off and shuts off the gas line. Note: the alarm mechanism has been removed. Value: $225

Clangor. 5-3/4" tall; 3-1/4" white dial. Thin bezel. Value: $125

C. (Manufactured by Ingraham Clock Co.) 3-3/4" paper dial; 6-1/4" nickel-plated case. I have no information what the C inside the shield stands for. Value: $125

Clangor. 5-3/4" tall; 3-1/4" white dial. Wide bezel. Value: $115

Colonial. 5-1/8" copper-plated tin case, brass ring and legs; 3-3/8" green tinted paper dial. Pat'd Dec. 3, 1912 to Jan. 14, 1913. Value: $95

Comet. 5-3/4" tall; 3-1/4" white paper dial. Thin bezel. Value: $125

Comet. 5-3/4" tall; 3-3/8" white paper dial. Wide bezel, shut off knob in ring. Value: $115

Commodore. (Manufactured by Ingraham Clock Co.) 3-1/4" paper dial; 6" nickel-plated case with brass top piece. Value: $115

Commodore. 5-3/4" blue painted case; 3-3/8" blue paper dial. Nickel ring and legs, shut off knob on ring. Value: $115

Dawn. 5" tall; 3-3/8" white dial. Pat'd Dec. 3, 1912 to Jan. 14, 1913. Shut off in ring. Mfg'd 5-29. Value: $95

Double Duty. 5" tall; 3-3/8" dial. Luminous numbers and hands. Mfg'd 2-37. Shut off inside ring. Value: $120

Erliup. 6-1/4" tall; 3-7/8" dial. Shut off lever on bell. Value: $150

Flyer. 6" tall; 3-3/8" white dial. Value: $125

Flyer. 5-7/8" tall; 3-1/4" white dial. Value: $125

Giant. 6-1/4" tall; 4" white dial. Thin bezel. Value: $115

Gem. 5-1/8" tall; 3-1/4" white dial. Shut off left side. Value: $100

Giant. (Manufactured by Ingraham Clock Co.) 4" black paper dial with luminous numbers and hands; 6" nickel-plated case. Alarm shut off upper left. Value: $175

Giant. 6-1/4" tall; 4" white dial. Wide bezel. Value: $100

Guard Eight Day. 7" tall; 4" white dial. Alarm shut off top, front of case. Value: $100

Indian. 5-1/2" tall; 3-3/4" white dial. Brass alarm shut off and legs. Pat'd Dec. 3, 1912 through Jan. 14, 1913. Value: $100

Indian. 5-3/4" tall; 3-3/4" white dial. Brass ring, alarm shut off and legs. Pat'd Dec. 3, 1912 through Jan. 14, 1913. Value: $125

Indian. 6" tall; 4" white dial. Alarm shut off inside ring. Mfg'd 11-34. Value: $140

Liberty, intermittent. 7" tall; 4" white dial. Alarm shut off in ring. Mfg'd 10-29. Value: $100

Intermittent Alarm

The rousing ring of this big alarm Clock will be sure to wake you up. The intermittent alarm is very insistent and if you are not fully aroused by his first call, he pauses a moment and starts off again until you do get up.

Compare this clock in size, quality and price with any other one-day alarm clock. It is 7 inches high, 2⅛ inches deep and has 4½-inch dial. Heavily nickel-plated brass dust-proof case. Runs thirty hours with one winding and has easy alarm shut-off at top. Shipping weight, 2 pounds 8 ounces.

46 G 1298—Plain dial......... $2.00
46 G 1299—Luminous dial..... 2.65

Liberty. 6-3/4" tall; 4" white dial. Shut off in top ring. Mfg'd 12-35. Value: $100

Macleco. 6-3/4" tall; 3-3/8" dial. Shut off in ring. Mfg'd 4-29. Value: $125

The National Call, 8 day alarm. 6-3/4" tall; 4" white dial. Value: $100

The National Call, 8 day alarm. 6-3/4" tall; 4" black dial. Luminous numbers and hands, shut off upper left. Mfg'd 1-39. Value: $125

The National Call, 8 day alarm. 6-3/4" tall; 4" white dial. Ivory painted case, nickel legs, ring, and shut off lever knob. Mfg'd 3-46. Value: $100

National Time Alarm. 7" tall; 4" white dial. Shut off in ring. Mfg'd 12-29. Value: $100

National Time Alarm. 7" tall; 4" black dial. Luminous numerals and hands. Mfg'd 12-35. Value: $125

Oak Leaf. 5-1/2" tall; 3-3/4" white dial. Piecrust bezel, shut off inside ring. In small letters on leaf reads: Wm. Enders St. Louis, USA. Pat'd Dec. 3, 1912 through Jan. 14, 1913. Value: $175

Sentinel. 6-1/4" tall; 3-3/4" silver paper dial. Alarm shut off top left. Value: $125

Sentinel. 6-1/4" tall; 3-3/4" white dial. Brass ring and legs. Value: $125

Signal. 5-3/4" tall; 3-3/8" white dial. Shut off in ring. Mfg'd 1-37. Value: $125

Standard. 6-3/4" tall; 4" white dial. Shut off in ring. Mfg'd 11-29. Value: $125

Victory Eight Day. 7" tall; 4" white dial. Shut off in ring. Value: $125

Super 8 Day. 7" tall; 4" black dial. Luminous numbers and hands. Value: $150

INGRAHAM CLOCKS

EIGHT-DAY ALARM CLOCKS

VICTORY

Height, 7 inches. Brass Case, nickeled and highly polished. Dial, 4½ inches in diameter. Large clear-toned bell on back.

No. 2381. Plain Dial, each **$5.70**

No. 2382. Luminous Dial, each **$7.17**

VICTORIAN RADIUM

Pedestal Clock. Height, 6½ inches. Case and pedestal nickeled and polished. Large clear-toned bell on back. Dial numerals and hands treated with a guaranteed radium preparation.

No. 2383. Plain Dial, each **$6.29**

No. 2384. Luminous Dial, each . . **$7.75**

ONE-DAY ALARM CLOCKS

LIBERTY

INTERMITTENT ALARM

Height, 7 inches. Nickeled and Polished. Large bell on back. Stem shut-off. Ten minute intermittent alarm.

No. 2385. Each **$3.65**

May be had with Radium dial. **No. 2385A**
Case Lots (24 clocks), each

59

LIBERATOR-RADIUM

PEDESTAL CLOCK

Height, 6½ inches. Case and pedestal Nickeled and Polished. Large bell on back. Stem shut-off. Intermittent alarm.

No. 2386.
Case Lots (24 clocks), each

May be had with white dial. **No. 2387.**

VIM. 5-1/4" tall; 3-1/4" white dial. Piecrust bezel. Pat'd Dec. 3, 1912 through Jan. 14, 1913. Value: $125

VIM. 5-1/8" tall; 3-1/4" white dial. Value: $95

VIM. 4-3/8" painted case; 3-3/8" white dial. Convex glass. Mfg'd 9-1935. Value: $75

Wards Old Reliable 8 Day. 7-1/8" tall; 4" white dial. Shut off in ring. Value: $100

Wards Old Reliable 8 Day. 7-1/8" tall; 4" black dial. Luminous numbers and hands. Mfg'd 6-29. Value: $125

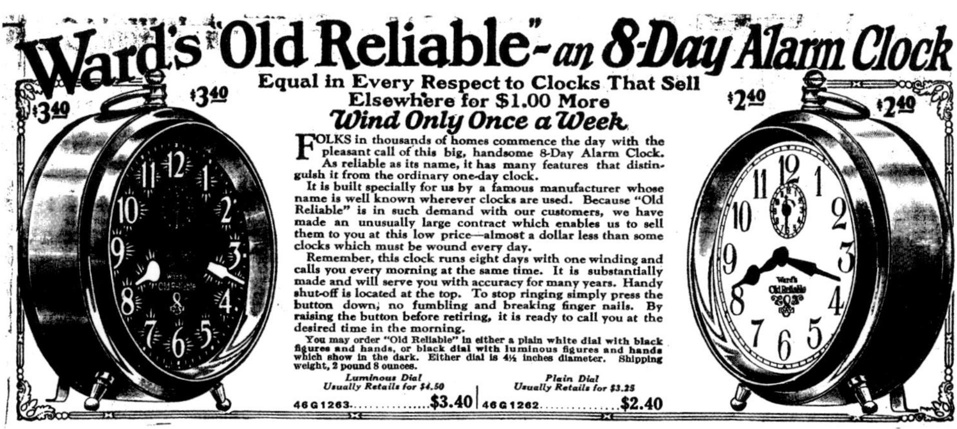

Lux

The Lux Clock Company was started in 1917 by Paul Lux, in Waterbury, Connecticut. Later, in 1950, he started a second plant in Lebanon, Tennessee. In 1961, the company was taken over by Robertshaw Fulton Controls.

Kitchenette. 5" tall; 3-1/2" dial. Dial is off-white and light green. Light green and ivory painted case. Red numbers indicate temperature. Brass knobs and legs. Value: $150

Overlook. 6-1/2" tall; 4" white dial. Alarm shut off top left with hand indicator on dial. Pat'd Apr. 27, 1920 on back; Pat'd 7-17-23 on dial. Value: $125

New Haven

The New Haven Clock Company originated in 1853 with Hiram Camp as President. They made movements for Jerome Mfg. Co., New Haven, Connecticut. The first clocks they produced in 1856 were one day and eight day O.G. clocks. They also produced smaller shelf clocks and alarm clocks.

In 1875 they made marine clocks that used a balance wheel control instead of a pendulum. Around 1880, they were producing back wind nickel alarms. Wristwatch movements were produced by 1915.

In 1929, the company started the production of electric clocks. By 1950 they were producing three million timepieces a year. Unfortunately, the New Haven Clock Company were out of business in 1959.

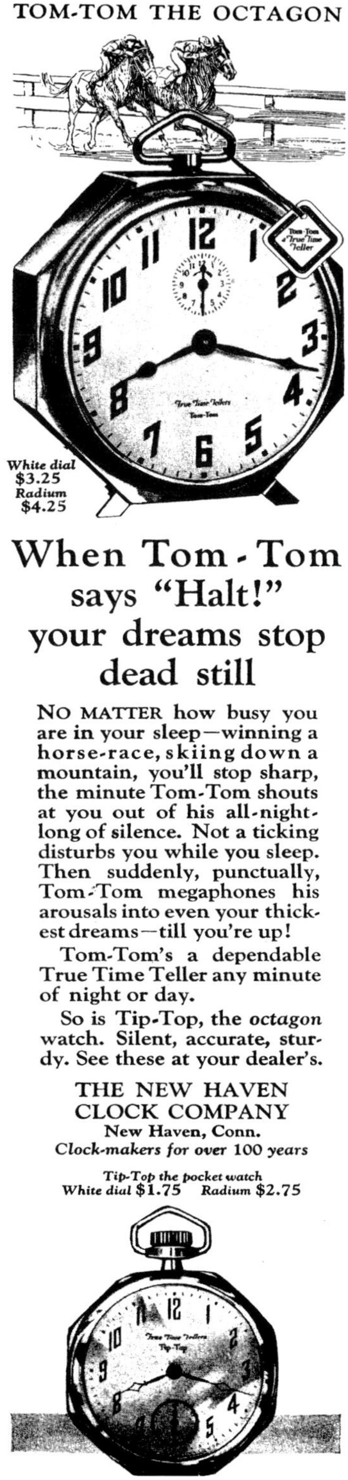

NEW HAVEN CLOCKS

NEW HAVEN ARTLARMS

"TAT-TOO JR." ARTLARM

Height, 2¾ inches; 2¼-inch Silvered Dial. Dependable 40-hour Movement. Back Bell Alarm with Shut-off. Seamless Metal Case with Moulded Base to match. Krack-Proof Krystal. Pastel Colors—Rose, Green, Yellow or Blue.

	Silvered Dial	Radium Dial
Broken Lots, each	$4.26	$5.62
Dozen Lots, each	4.16	5.52
Case Lots of 24, each	4.06	5.42

TIDY-TOT

Height, 3⅜ inches; Width, 2¾ inches; 2¼-inch Dial. Krack-Proof Krystal. Nickel-plated Octagon Case. 40-hour Movement. Back Bell, Intermittent Alarm with Shut-off.

	Silvered Dial	Radium Dial
Broken Lots, each	$4.60	$5.94
Dozen Lots, each	4.48	5.84
Case Lots of 24, each	4.38	5.74

TICK-TOCK

Height, 4¼ inches; 3¾-inch Dial. Dependable 40-hour Movement. Back Bell Alarm with Shut-off. Seamless Metal Case with Moulded Base to match. Convex Krack-Proof Krystal. Pastel Colors—Blue, Green, Yellow or Rose.

	White Dial	Radium Dial
Broken Lots, each	$3.54	$4.90
Dozen Lots, each	3.44	4.80
Case Lots of 24, each	3.34	4.70

The Alarm Clocks Beautiful

"TAT-TOO" ARTLARM

Height, 5 inches; 4½-inch Dial. Dependable 40-hour Movement. Back Bell Alarm with Shut-off. Seamless Metal Case with Moulded Base to match. Convex Krack-Proof Krystal. Green Pastel Finish.

	White Dial
Broken Lots, each	$4.26
Dozen Lots, each	4.16
Case Lots of 24, each	4.06

"TAT-TOO" ARTLARM, Radium

Height, 5 inches; 4½-inch Dial. Dependable 40-hour Movement, Back Bell Alarm with Shut-off. Seamless Metal Case with Moulded Base to match. Convex Krack-Proof Krystal. Green Pastel Finish.

	Radium Dial
Broken Lots, each	$5.62
Dozen Lots, each	5.52
Case Lots of 24, each	5.42

NEW HAVEN CLOCKS

DRESSER AND NOVELTY CLOCKS

"MOROCCO"

Dependable 8 Day Jeweled Movement in Handsome Leather Folding Traveling Case, Stem Wind, Stem Set. Silver Etched Radium Dial, Convex Crystal. Visible Regulator. Green, Pink, Blue, Tan or Black $21.00

"ROVENA"

Height, 4 inches, Width 3¼ inches. Dependable 8 Day Movement. Metal Case with Buffed Sash. Silvered Dial with Second Hand. Beveled Convex Crystal. Case Finished in a Rich French Bronze. $11.25

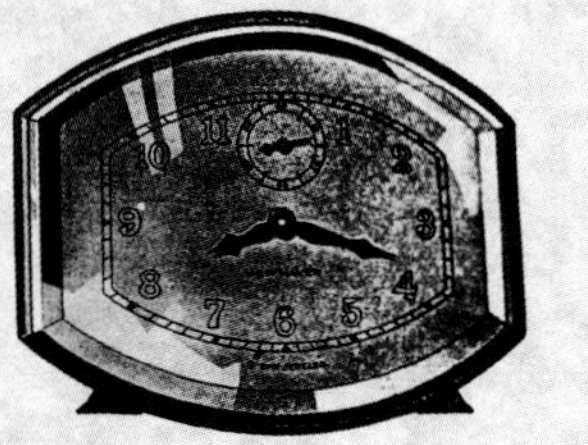

"FAYETTE"

Height, 2⅞ inches. Width, 3½ inches. Dependable 8 Day Jeweled Movement. Silvered Metal Case with Easel Rest. Beveled Glass Crystal, Silvered Dial with Radium Hands and Numerals. $21.00

"AIGRETTE"

Height, 3½ inches. 40-hour Movement, 2 inch Dial. Raised Numerals. Three-Ply Pentagon Case of 3 Colors, furnished in Pearl, Blue, Pink or Green. Bowed Crystal. $3.44

"TIP-TOP TRAVELER"

Height, 1⅞ inches. Silvered Radium Dial. Second Hand. Pull-out Set, Stem Wind. Nickel-plated Octagon Case. Bowed Crystal $4.76

"ELDORE"

Height, 2¼ inches. Width, 2¼ inches. Dependable 40-hour Movement, Metal Case of Attractive Design. Bowed Krack-Proof Krystal. White Dial, Pastel Colors, Rose, Green or Blue. $2.70

"ESTELLE"

Height, 2⅝ inches. Width 2¼ inches. Dependable 40-hour Movement, Metal Case of Gothic Design. Bowed Krack-Proof Krystal, White Dial. Pastel Colors, Rose, Green or Blue. $2.70

"ICOT,"

Height, 3½ inches. Width 8 inches. Moulded Case, 2½ inch Silvered Dial. 40-hour Movement. Mahogany Finish.

Timepiece, Silvered Dial $5.30
Alarm, Silvered Dial $6.65
Alarm, Radium Dial $8.00

"IOTA"

Height, 2½ inches. Width, 5½ inches. 40-hour Movement, 2 inch Silvered Dial. Raised Numerals. Mahogany, Red or Walnut Moulded Case $4.16

"IDOLE"

Height, 4 inches. Width, 8 inches. Mahogany Finished Case with Two-Toned Panels.

Timepiece, Silvered Dial $5.30
Alarm, Silvered Dial $6.65

"IBIS"

Height, 4 inches. Width, 8 inches. Mahogany Finished Case with Two-Toned Panels.

Timepiece, Silvered Dial $5.30
Alarm, Silvered Dial $6.65

All Right Rackett (barely visible in oval below hand shaft). 7-1/2" tall; 3-3/4" white dial. Pat'd Nov. 29, 1898. Value: $125

The Automatic Alarm 8 Days (red letters). 7-1/2" tall; 3-3/4" white dial. Narrow hand is alarm set. Pat'd Oct. 20, 1908. I have seen this available in nickel, copper, brass, silver, and antique copper finishes. Dials available in either Roman or Arabic. Value: $125

Automatic Alarm. Correct Time Co. (New Haven Clock Co.) 7-1/2" tall; 3-7/8" dial. Shut off on right on back. Pat'd Oct. 20, 1908. Value: $125

Ben Hur. 6-1/2" tall; 3-1/4" white dial. Brass top ring and legs, alarm shut off on bell. Mfg'd for Farwell, Ozmun, Kirk & Co., St. Paul, Minn. Value: $150

The Cascade. 4-3/8" tall; 1-3/4" white dial. Second bit, brass case, cast top piece and legs. Time only. Value: $125

Brownie. 4" tall; 2-1/8" white dial. Alarm shut off top right, steady repeat top left. Value: $110

The Giant (red letters intermittent). 7-3/8" tall; 4-5/8" white dial. Brass case, pat'd Nov. 29, 1898. Value: $225

Intermittent. 6-1/4" tall; 3-7/8" white dial. Value: $110

Jumbo Wireless (red letters), intermittent. Correct Time Co. (New Haven) 7-7/8" tall; 3-3/4" white dial. Copper-plated brass case. Pat'd Nov. 29, 1898. Value: $125

Junior Tattoo (red letters). 3" tall; 1-3/4" white dial. Pat'd Apr. 5, '04. Value: $110

The Junior Tattoo. 3" tall; 1-3/4" white dial. Piecrust bezel, pat'd April 5, 1904. Value: $135

The Junior Tattoo Radium. 3" tall, 1-3/4" black dial. Luminous numbers and hands. Pat'd Apr. 5, '04. Value: $135

Junior Tattoo (red letters). 3-1/4" tall; 1-3/4" white dial. Different top, pat'd Apr. 5, '04. 12/21/17 scratched on back. Value: $125

Junior Wireless, intermittent, Correct Time Co. (New Haven) 5" tall; 2-3/8" white dial. Porcelain dial, copper-plated brass case. Pat'd Apr. 5, '04. Value: $150

Marathon 8 Day (red letters), Correct Time Co. (New Haven) 7-3/8" tall; 3-7/8" white dial. Narrow hand is alarm set. Pat'd Oct. 20, 1908. Value: $125

Marathon 8 Day Automatic Alarm. 7-7/8" tall; 3-3/4" black dial. Luminous numbers and hands, narrow hand is alarm set. Pat'd Oct. 20, 1908. Value: $150

O V B Our Very Best, H.S.B. & Co. 6-1/4" tall; 4-1/8" white dial. Narrow hand is alarm set, alarm shut off on top of case. Window in dial indicates "Will Ring". Value: $150

Rapid Fire. 6" tall; 3-3/4" white dial. Brass case, pat'd Nov. 29, 1898. Value: $100

Slumber Stopper, Radium. 5-1/4" tall; 3-1/2" white dial. Luminous numbers and hands, shut off on top behind ring. Value: $150

The Tattoo Intermittent. 5-3/4" tall; 3-3/4" white dial. Piecrust bezel, The Tattoo printed in red, shut off on back. Value: $135

The Tattoo Luminous Intermittent. 6-1/4" tall; 4" luminous dial. Appears entire dial was luminous. Alarm indicator on back bell, shut off on top of back, top; piecrust bezel. Pat'd 1897. Value: $150

The Tattoo (red letters). 6-1/4" tall; 3-7/8" white dial. Pat'd Nov. 29, 1898. Value: $125

The Tattoo (red letters), intermittent. 6" tall; 3-7/8" white dial. Shut off on top behind top piece. 9-26-22 scratched on back. Value: $125

Tidy Tot. 3-1/4" tall; 2-1/8" white dial. Value: $100

Tidy Tot. 3-1/2" tall; 2-1/8" white dial. Brass case. Value: $110

Tidy Tot. 3-1/2" tall; 2-1/8" black dial. Luminous numbers and hands. Value: $125

Tidy Tot. 3-1/2" tall; 2-1/4" white dial. Painted ivory case. Value: $90

Tip Top Traveler. 1-1/8" metal silver dial; 2" tall. Luminous hands and numerals, pat'd June 3, '24. Shown with original box. Value: $110

Tom Tom. 5-1/2" tall; 4" white dial. Convex glass. Value: $125

Tom Tom. 6" tall; 4" white dial. Convex glass. 5-11-28 scratched on case. Value: $125

True Time Tellers (Manufactured by New Haven Clock Co.) 2-1/8" silver-plated dial; 3-1/2" nickel-plated case. Value: $95

Wizard Intermittent. 6" tall; 3-7/8" white dial. Wizard printed in red. Marswells. Sold by Marshall Wells Co. Pat'd Nov. 29, 1898. Value: $115

Wizard Intermittent. 6" tall; 3-3/4" white dial. Wizard printed in red. Correct Time Co. (New Haven) Value: $125

New Haven Clock Co. 6-1/4" tall; 3-1/4" white dial. Brass legs and ring, scratched on back, cleaned and repaired. Oct. 3, 1889 $1.25. Value: $125

New Haven USA. 6-1/4" tall; 3-3/8" white dial. Value: $125

New Haven Clock Co. 6-1/4" tall; 3-3/8" white dial. Value: $125

New Haven Clock Co. 6-1/4" tall; 4-1/8" white dial. Narrow hand is alarm set, shut off top of case. Window in dial indicates WILL RING. Value: $135

New Haven USA. 6-1/4" tall; 3-1/4" white calendar dial. Piecrust bezel, brass legs and ring. Top appears not original. Alarm set on back, pat'd April 6, 1897. Value: $175

New Haven Clock Co. 3" tall; 1-3/4" white dial. Piecrust bezel, pat'd April 5, 1904. Value: $115

The Wireless (red letters) Intermittent. Correct Time Company (New Haven) Private label dial, Oriska Hdwe, Imp't Co. Oriska, No. Dak. 6-5/8" tall; 3-7/8" white dial. Copper-plated brass case with brass top piece and legs. Pat'd Nov. 29, 1890. Value: $175

The Wireless (red letters) Intermittent. Marswells. Sold by Marshall Wells Co. Private label dial. Nerseth & Fauchald White Earth, N.D. 6-5/8" tall; 3-7/8" white dial. Antique copper finish, brass case. Pat'd Nov. 29, 1898. Value: $175

Parker

The Parker Clock Co. of Meriden, Connecticut, took over the Parker & Whipple Co. in 1893. They manufactured small pendulum desk clocks and soon started producing round alarm clocks. The Parker Co. was also well known for their excellent marine clocks. The company was dissolved in 1934.

Hallmark. 6-1/2" tall; 3-3/4" white dial. Alarm knobs on top of case. Left arm-silent alarm; right knob steady repeat. Patents Nov. 16, 1897-Nov. 25, 1913. Value: $125

Hallmark. 6-1/2" tall; 4" white dial. Top piece believed not to be original. Value: $125

Mammoth. (Manufactured by Parker Clock Co.) 5" paper dial; 7-1/2" nickel-plated case, top handle not original. Pat'd Nov. 16, 1897, Dec. 29, 1903. Value: $250

Radium. 5-1/2" tall; 3-3/4" black dial. Luminous numbers and hands. Scratched on back: Sold 3-9-1920. Value: $150

Parker Trade Mark Patented Alarm. 5-7/8" tall; 3-3/4" white dial. Extra hand on dial is alarm set hand. Pat'd Nov. 16, 1897 to Dec. 29, 1903. Value: $125

Parker. (Manufactured by Parker Clock Co.) 1-11/16" celluloid dial; 3" solid brass case. Slightly convex beveled glass. Value: $125

Parker. 5-7/8" tall; 3-3/4" white dial. Alarm shut off upper left, Parker trade mark stamped on back. Value: $125

Parker Clock Co. 5-1/4" tall; 3-1/2" white dial. Center alarm dial. Value: $110

Parker Clock Co.
Private label dial. Edwin Pape Jeweler Davenport, Iowa. 7-3/8" tall; 5" white dial. Repeat option on back, pat'd Nov. 16, 1897 to Dec. 29, 1903. Value: $175

Scott

I have no information on the Scott Clock Corp. The clock has a very fine movement.

Minute Alarm. 6-3/4" tall; 4" white dial. Two alarm dials, top to set the hour, bottom to set the minute. Pat'd Aug. 29, 1916 to Nov. 29, 1921. Value: $150

Sessions

William E. Sessions purchased the Welch Clock Co. in 1903. The company was known as The Sessions Clock Co. in Bristol, Connecticut. Mr. Sessions reorganized the company and made it one of the largest modern producers of Connecticut clocks.

Colonial. 6-1/2" tall; 4" white dial. Shut off upper right, on-off window. Top piece is not original. Value: $150

Columbia. 7-1/8" tall; 4" white dial. Shut off upper right, on-off window. Pat'd Dec. 31, 1912. Value: $100

Columbia Radium. 7-1/8" tall; 4" black dial. Luminous numbers and hands. Pat'd Dec. 31, 1912. Shut off upper right, on-off window. Value: $125

Dependable 8 day alarm. (Manufactured by Sessions Clock Co.) 4" paper dial; 6-3/4" nickel-plated case. Alarm shut off knob upper right with on-off window. Pat'd Dec. 31, 1912. Value: $135

The National Call. 7" tall; 4" white dial. Pat'd Dec. 31, 1912. Shut off upper right, on-off window. Value: $100

The National Call. 6-3/4" tall; 4" white dial. Shut off upper right, no on-off window. Pat'd Dec. 31, 1912. Value: $100

Solus. 7-1/8" tall; 4" white dial. Shut off upper right, on-off window. Pat'd Dec. 31, 1912. Value: $100

8 Day Alarm. 7-1/8" tall; 4" white dial. Shut off upper right, on-off window. Pat'd Dec. 31, 1912. Value: $100

Seth Thomas

The Seth Thomas Clock Co. was first organized in Plymouth Hollow, Connecticut, in 1813. In 1866, Plymouth Hollow changed its name to Thomaston, in honor of Seth Thomas. Around 1875 they were producing round alarm clocks.

In 1930, the company became a part of General Time, and in 1949 changed their name to The General Time Corp. The year 2001 saw another change, when Colibri Group of Providence, Rhode Island, bought Seth Thomas and all trademarks.

8-1/4" brass case; 4-1/4" white dial with second bit. One piece case, piecrust bezel. Alarm on back. Value: $250

Seth Thomas. 6-1/2" tall; 3-3/4" white dial. Seconds bit, brass legs, ring, and knobs. Value: $150

Seth Thomas. 6-1/2" tall; 3-3/4" white dial. Seconds bit, change of lettering style. Value: $150

Seth Thomas. 4-1/2" tall; 1-3/4" white dial. Celluloid case, brass ring, bezel, and legs. Time only. Value: $175

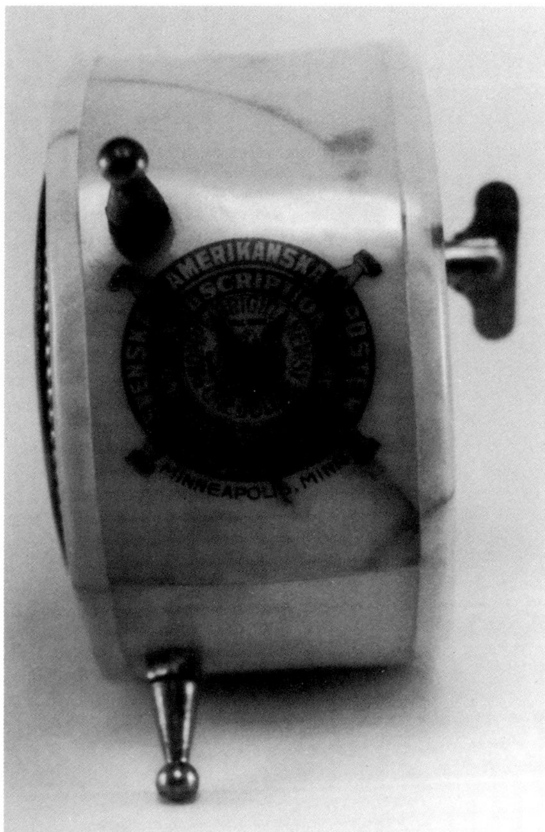

Bottom label subscription premium from: Svenska Amerikanska Posten Subscription Full Value Only One Dollar Prompt Bright Newsy One Dollar per Year Swan J. Turnblad Publ. Minneapolis, Minn.

Premier Alarm

Nickel Finish.
One-day Continuous Alarm.
Dial, 4¼ inches.

Height, 6⅞ inches.

Silver Colored Dial.
also
Black Dial.
Radium Numerals and Hands.

Case lots (24 clocks) $3.36
Broken lots (less than 24 clocks) 3.54

Radium, case lots (24 clocks) $4.66
Radium, broken lots (less than 24 clocks) 5.10

Thrift Alarm

Colors: Red, Blue, Green, Yellow or Nickel.
One-day Time. Continuous Alarm. Seamless Case. 3¾-inch Silvered Dial. Height, 6 inches.

Case lots (50 clocks) $1.50

Broken lots (less than 50 clocks) $1.60

Rouser Alarm

Colors: Red, Blue, Green, Yellow or Nickel.
One-day Time. Continuous Alarm. Seamless Case. 4-inch Silvered Dial. Height, 5¼ inches. Alarm hammer striking inside of case.

Case lots (50 clocks) $1.50
Broken lots (less than 50 clocks) 1.60

Black Dial, Radium hands. Case lots (50 clocks) $2.02
Broken lots (less than 50 clocks) 2.12

KEYSTONE LIST PRICES

Waterbury

Waterbury Clock Co. was organized in Waterbury, Connecticut, on March 27, 1857, as a branch of Benedict and Burnham. A new factory was built on Elm St. in 1873. By 1892 they began manufacturing watches for Ingersoll. The company was purchased by Robert H. Ingersoll and his brother in 1914. In 1944, the firm became U.S. Time Corp.

Autodraft Mfg. Co. New York City. 5-3/4" tall; 3-3/8" white dial. Pat'd Nov. 29, 1910 through June 7, 1921. Value: $175

Call. 6" tall; 3-5/8" white dial. Pat'd Nov. 29, 1910 through Jan. 29, 1918. Value: $125

Call Boy. 5-1/2" tall; 3-1/4" white dial. Copper-plated brass case. Value: $110

Cyclone. 6-3/4" tall; 4-1/8" white dial. Silent alarm knob on top right, long and repeat knob on top left. Pat'd March 15, 1898 through April 25, 1911. Value: $115

Daybreak. (Manufactured by Waterbury Clock Co.) 3-5/8" paper dial; 5-7/8" nickel-plated case. Unusual top piece, pat'd Oct. 29, 1907, Jan. 29, 1918. Value: $125

Gale. 4-1/2" tall; 2" white dial. Long and repeat knob on top left, silent knob on top right. Pat'd June 4, 1907 through Jan. 29, 1918. Value: $100

Giant Spasmodic. 7" tall; 4-5/8" white dial. Alarm shut off on back. Patents Jan. 29, 1901 through Jan. 29, 1907. Value: $150

Luminous. 6-1/2" tall; 3-1/4" white dial. Appears entire dial was luminous. Seconds bit, alarm set on back. Patents March 19, 1889 through Jan. 29, 1901. Value: $150

Spasmodic. 5-3/4" tall; 3-3/4" white dial. Pat'd Jan. 29, 1907 through Jan. 29, 1918. Value: $125

Spasmodic. 5-1/2" tall; 3-3/4" white dial. Patents Jan. 29, 1907 through Jan. 2, 1923. Value: $125

Spasmodic Alarm. 5-5/8" tall; 4" white dial. Pat'd March 15, 1898. Extremely narrow bezel. Value: $175

Spasmodic Alarm. 5-3/4" tall; 3-3/4" white dial. Shown with original box, pat'd March 15, 1898. Date scratched on back 7/2/1901 A.L. Value: $175

Spasmodic Alarm. 5-3/4" tall; 3-5/8" white dial. Pat'd Mar. 15, 1898 through Jan. 29, 1907. Value: $125

Spasmodic Alarm. 6" tall; 3-3/4" white dial. Patents Mar. 15, 1898 through Jan. 29, 1907. Value: $125

Thrift. 5" tall; 3-1/2" white dial. Pat'd Oct. 29, 1907 through Jan. 29, 1918. Value: $115

Thrift. 6" tall; 3-3/8" white dial. Known as nickel, copper, and painted cases. Pat'd Nov. 29, 1910 through June 7, 1921. Value: $125

Thrift. 6" tall; 3-3/8" white dial. Pat'd Jan. 29, 1918 through June 15, 1922. Value: $125

Turnout. Private label dial. C.R. Runkle Jeweler Lisbon, Iowa. 6-1/4" tall; 3-5/8" white dial. Pat'd Jan. 29, 1901 through Nov. 29, 1910. Value: $175

Valory. 6" tall; 3-1/2" gold paper dial. Pat'd Nov. 29, 1910 through June 7, 1921. Value: $125

Vanitie. 6-1/4" tall; 3-7/8" white dial. Pat'd Jan. 29, 1918. Value: $115

Varsity. 5-3/8" tall; 3-1/2" gold paper dial. Pat'd Jan. 29, 1918. Value: $100

Victor X-Ray Corporation, Interval Timer Chicago, Ill. 5-5/8" tall; 2-1/4" white dial. Outer ring minute timer, inner ring hour timer. Set timer up to two hours. When lever is pulled down, clock runs. When clock zero's out, alarm rings and stops clock. Value: $125

Vigilant. 5-1/4" tall; 3-1/2" white dial. Pat'd Jan. 29, 1901. Should be flat glass, scratched on back: Bought in March 1916 from F.L. Brown Jewelry by Geo. R. Roelke Price $1.50. Value: $100

Vigilant. 5-1/4" tall; 3-1/2" white dial. Shown with original box. Pat'd Jan. 29, 1918. Value: $175

Vigilant. 5-7/8" tall; 3-1/2" white dial. Pat'd Jan. 29, 1918 through June 15, 1920. Scratched on back: 1-4-23. Value: $125

Ware-Well. 5-3/4" tall; 3-1/2" white dial. Brass ring, pat'd Nov. 29, 1910 through June 7, 1921. Value: $125

Westinghouse. 7-1/8" tall; 4-1/8" white dial. Pat'd Jan. 29, 1907 through Apr. 25, 1911. Value: $175

Waterbury Clock Co. Private label dial. Emerick & Barrett Jewelers & Opticians Freeport, Ills. 6-1/4" tall; 3-1/2" white dial. Seconds bit, alarm set on back. Pat'd Jan. 29, 1901. Value: $175

Waterbury Clock Co. Private label dial. Edwin P. Long Jeweler St. Cloud, Minn. 6" tall; 3-1/4" white dial. Seconds bit, alarm set on back. Pat'd Jan. 29, 1901. Value: $175

Waterbury Clock Co. 3" tall; 1-11/16" white dial. Brass ring and legs, scratched on back: 11/05 B & Co. Value: $100

Waterbury Clock Co. 3-1/8" tall; 1-11/16" white dial. Brass ring and legs, pat'd Mar. 15, 1888 through Feb. 19, 1901. Value: $100

Waterbury Clock Co. 3" tall; 1-11/16" white dial. Brass case, pat'd May 6, 1890 through May 29, 1894. Value: $100

Waterbury Clock Co. 3-3/4" paper dial; 5-1/2" nickel-plated case. Another different top piece, narrow bezel. Pat'd Mar. 15, 1898, Jan. 29, 1901. Value: $125

Waterbury Clock Co. 6" tall; 3-1/4" white dial. Seconds bit, alarm set on back. Pat'd Jan. 29, 1901 through June 16, 1908. Value: $125

Waterbury Clock Co. 6" tall; 3-3/8" white dial. Case is painted dark red. Pat'd Nov. 29, 1910 through June 7, 1921. Value: $110

Welch

E.N. Welch began The Welch Mfg. Co. in Bristol, Connecticut, in 1864. The company went into receivership in 1897 and became the Sessions Clock Co. in 1903.

E.N. Welch Mfg. Co. 6-1/2" tall; 3-1/4" white dial. Hammered brass case. Value: $150

Westclox

Western Clock Mfg. Co. originated in Peru, Illinois, in 1887. The company changed the name to Western Clock Co. in 1895. The Westclox name first appeared around 1910. The company became the largest producer of alarm clocks in the United States. Big Ben first appeared on the market in 1908. Later, in 1912, we started to see Baby Ben appear.

Westclox became a division of General Time Instruments Corp. in 1934, and continues under that name today.

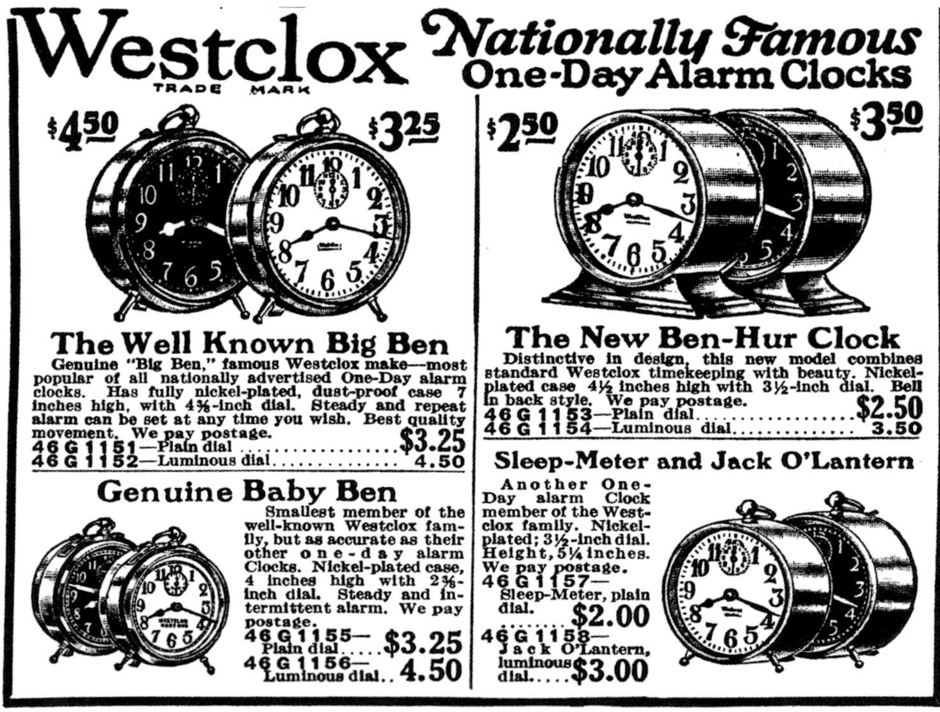

Westclox *Big Ben* - *just tell him when*

MAYBE you swear at him some mornings when you'd give anything in the world for forty winks more!

But, after all, you swear *by* him because he's only carrying out your own orders and calling you exactly when you say.

And isn't that what you want? A clock that takes time seriously; that lets you sleep right up to the last tick; and then keeps good time all day.

Right there's the reason why Westclox alarms have so many friends: they run and ring on time. Why shouldn't they? Every Westclox has that same good construction that got Big Ben up in the world.

Western Clock Co.—makers of Westclox

La Salle and Peru, Ill., U. S. A.

Westclox

Big Ben—for a fatter pay envelope

WONDERFUL how that fellow, Big Ben, can help bring things your way when pay-raise time comes around. Maybe it's because the boss has a clock just like yours and is johnny on the spot himself.

That's part of Big Ben's job: helping his friends get up in the world.

All Westclox have this knack: punctuality is second nature with them. Each clock must be up to snuff before it can leave the factory. It must earn the right to wear that Westclox quality mark of good timekeeping.

Big Ben is the best known of the Westclox group. He and Baby Ben have been favorites for years. Sleep-Meter, on the market but a few years, has stepped right to the front. And the *America*—the oldest Westclox—still outsells them all.

Whichever clock you choose, you'll like. They're all Westclox and made *right* to make good.

WESTERN CLOCK CO., LA SALLE, ILLINOIS, U. S. A.

Makers of *Westclox*: Big Ben, Baby Ben, Pocket Ben, Glo-Ben, America, Sleep-Meter, Jack o' Lantern

Factory: Peru, Illinois. *In Canada*: Western Clock Co., Ltd., Peterborough, Ont.

THE SATURDAY EVENING POST

Westclox

—that's Big Ben's family name

Classmates of Big Ben

OUT of the Westclox school of good timekeeping at La Salle, Illinois, has come a class of alarm clocks that people everywhere respect.

Each clock bears Big Ben's family name—Westclox—on the dial and tag. This means that it has learned its lesson well.

The final examinations at the Big Ben school of punctuality are hard to pass. No clock can get out into the world with a Westclox diploma until its makers are satisfied it will be a credit to them.

The *America* alarm—the one with the top-bell—belonged to the class of '86. Think of it! On the job now for nearly thirty-five years and still going strong. This, of course, is Big Ben's oldest brother—pioneer of that good Westclox construction method.

Sleep-Meter was of the class of '14—a sturdy, friendly timekeeper and alarm that stepped quickly to the front in the alarm clock field.

Pocket Ben is that good, serviceable, two-dollar watch you've heard about. He has a double, reinforced back that makes him all the more dependable. Look up Pocket Ben at your dealer's first chance you get.

WESTERN CLOCK CO., LA SALLE, ILLINOIS, U. S. A.

Makers of *Westclox:* Big Ben, Baby Ben, Pocket Ben, Glo-Ben, America, Sleep-Meter, Jack o' Lantern

Factory: Peru, Illinois. *In Canada:* Western Clock Co., Limited, Peterborough, Ont.

2 The American Magazine

Westclox

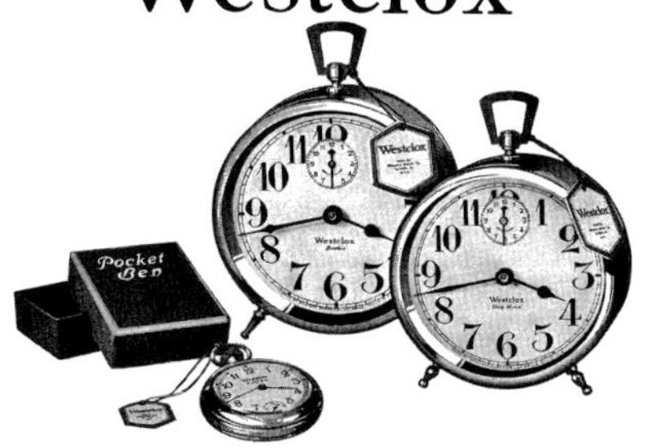

For sound restful sleep

WHETHER we are ready to rise at the tap of the gong, or whether we long to roll over and forget the world in one long, comfortable snooze, it gives us a better start for the day if we have ample time to dress, breakfast and get to our business.

Those who ride in early cars and have perfect punctuality records are likely to rise to a Westclox tuneful call. They sleep soundly, restfully, confident that their Westclox will rouse them punctually.

For every Westclox alarm is trained to run on time, ring on time, stay on time. It starts with the selection of the material, through every operation, till the finished timepiece is given a running test to prove its right to wear the name Westclox on its dial and orange-bordered, six-sided buff tag.

And Pocket Ben, a watch, keeps good time in the pocket. A watch that is worthy to wear the Westclox name and tag.

WESTERN CLOCK CO., LA SALLE, ILLINOIS, U. S. A.

Factory: Peru, Illinois. *In Canada:* Western Clock Co., Limited, Peterbbrough, Ont.

Westclox *Big Ben* — 7 inches tall. 4½-inch dial. Runs 32 hours. Steady and intermittent alarm, $3.50. In Canada, $4.50.

Westclox *Baby Ben* — 3¾ inches tall. 2½-inch dial. Runs 32 hours. Steady and intermittent alarm, $3.50. In Canada, $4.50.

Westclox *America* — 6½ inches tall. 4-inch dial. Nickel case. Runs 32 hours. Top bell alarm, $1.50. In Canada, $2.00.

Westclox *Jack o' Lantern* — 5 inches tall. Luminous dial and hands. Back bell alarm. Runs 32 hours, $3.00. In Canada, $4.00.

Westclox *Sleep-Meter* — 5 inches tall. Nickeled case. 4-inch dial. Back bell alarm. Runs 32 hours, $2.00. In Canada, $3.00.

Westclox *Pocket Ben* — A nickel plated watch. Stem wind and set. Neat hands and dial. Dependable, $1.50. In Canada, $2.00.

Westclox *Glo-Ben* — Nickel plated watch. Stem wind and set. Black face, luminous dial and hands, $2.50. In Canada, $3.50.

Westclox

Days in and nights out

IT'S all the same to Westclox whether you prepare to tuck away four hours of beauty sleep or meet the night shift on their way home.

Getting-in time is your own affair, but when getting-up time rolls around Westclox make themselves heard.

For folks who get in when they please and get up when they must, Westclox are friends indeed.

Of course they butt in on a sound sleep at its most delightful moment, but they work under your orders. If you ask them to call you they do it punctually, cheerfully, tunefully.

You will find Westclox alarms in several sizes and prices. Each one must run on time and ring on time before it can wear the trade mark Westclox on its face.

Pocket Ben, a watch bearing the Westclox trade mark, furnishes dependable time for the pocket.

WESTERN CLOCK CO., LA SALLE, ILLINOIS, U. S. A.

Factory: Peru, Illinois. *In Canada:* Western Clock Co., Limited, Peterborough, Ont.

Westclox *Big Ben* — 7 inches tall. 4½-inch dial. Runs 32 hours. Steady and intermittent alarm, $3.50. In Canada, $4.50.

Westclox *Baby Ben* — 3¾ inches tall. 2¾-inch dial. Runs 32 hours. Steady and intermittent alarm, $3.50. In Canada, $4.50.

Westclox *America* — 6¾ inches tall. 4-inch dial. Nickel case. Runs 32 hours. Top bell alarm, $1.50. In Canada, $2.00.

Westclox *Jack o' Lantern* — 5 inches tall. Luminous dial and hands. Back bell alarm. Runs 32 hours, $3.00. In Canada, $4.00.

Westclox *Sleep-Meter* — 5 inches tall. Nickeled case. 4-inch dial. Back bell alarm. Runs 32 hours, $2.00. In Canada, $3.00.

Westclox *Pocket Ben* — A nickel plated watch. Stem wind and set. Neat hands and dial. Dependable, $1.50. In Canada, $2.00.

Westclox *Glo-Ben* — Nickel plated watch. Stem wind and set. Black face, luminous dial and hands, $2.50. In Canada, $3.50.

Westclox

In the dead of night

"SCARCELY breathing, he watched the slight movement of the curtain. The cold stare of an automatic held his eye. In a flash—"

The clock on the stair booms the hour. Bedtime. But who is going to leave the hero in a fix like that?

On and on you and the hero pursue adventures, and round and round creep the hands of the clock.

When you do turn in, hours past your bedtime, put your confidence in the Westclox by your bedside.

Evening hours may pass unheeded by you and the hero. There's a morning hour that must not slip by unnoticed. So ask your trusty Westclox to call you on the dot.

Westclox are made to run on time, to ring on time, to stay on time. You can choose them by the trade mark Westclox on the dial and orange-bordered tag.

WESTERN CLOCK CO., LA SALLE, ILLINOIS, U. S. A.

Factory: Peru, Illinois. *In Canada:* Western Clock Co., Limited, Peterborough, Ont.

Westclox *Big Ben* — 7 inches tall. 4½-inch dial. Runs 32 hours. Steady and intermittent alarm, $3.50. In Canada, $4.50.

Westclox *Baby Ben* — 3¾ inches tall. 2¾-inch dial. Runs 32 hours. Steady and intermittent alarm, $3.50. In Canada, $4.50.

Westclox *America* — 6¾ inches tall. 4-inch dial. Nickel case. Runs 32 hours. Top bell alarm, $1.50. In Canada, $2.00.

Westclox *Jack o' Lantern* — 5 inches tall. Luminous dial and hands. Back bell alarm. Runs 32 hours, $3.00. In Canada, $4.00.

Westclox *Sleep-Meter* — 5 inches tall. Nickeled case. 4-inch dial. Back bell alarm. Runs 32 hours, $2.00. In Canada, $3.00.

Westclox *Pocket Ben* — A nickel plated watch. Stem wind and set. Neat hands and dial. Dependable, $1.50. In Canada, $2.00.

Westclox *Glo-Ben* — Nickel plated watch. Stem wind and set. Black face, luminous dial and hands, $2.50. In Canada, $3.50.

Westclox

Up late at night, on time in the morning

THERE are so many things to tempt us to stay up at night, and usually only one thing to get us out in the morning.

And few of us look forward to getting up as we do to staying up.

That is the reason for Westclox—to see that we wake on time, for no matter how late we are in getting to bed, our getting up time must be the same every day.

When our faithful Westclox rings us out of a sound sleep, we may be inclined to be peevish until we remember that our faith in our Westclox enabled us to enjoy that sound, comfortable slumber.

Before an alarm clock can earn the right to wear the trade mark Westclox on its dial and tag, it must prove its ability to run on time, ring on time, and stay on time.

You will find Westclox alarms and watches at most good stores. Look for the orange-bordered, six-sided tag and the Westclox on the dial.

WESTERN CLOCK CO., LA SALLE, ILLINOIS, U. S. A.

Factory: Peru, Illinois. *In Canada:* Western Clock Co., Limited, Peterborough, Ont.

Westclox *Big Ben* 7 inches tall. 4½-inch dial. Runs 32 hours. Steady and intermittent alarm, $3.50. In Canada, $4.50.

Westclox *Baby Ben* 3¾ inches tall. 2¾-inch dial. Runs 32 hours. Steady and intermittent alarm, $3.50. In Canada, $4.50.

Westclox *America* 6½ inches tall. 4-inch dial. Nickel case. Runs 32 hours. Top bell alarm, $1.50. In Canada, $2.00.

Westclox *Jack o'Lantern* 5 inches tall. Luminous dial and hands. Back bell alarm. Runs 32 hours, $3.00. In Canada, $4.00.

Westclox *Sleep-Meter* 5 inches tall. Nickeled case. 4-inch dial. Back bell alarm. Runs 32 hours, $2.00. In Canada, $3.00.

Westclox *Pocket Ben* A nickel plated watch. Stem wind and set. Neat hands and dial. Dependable, $1.50. In Canada, $2.00.

Westclox *Glo-Ben* Nickel plated watch. Stem wind and set. Black face, luminous dial and hands, $2.50. In Canada, $3.50.

Westclox

The last place to go

MOTORING at night—the engine purrs contentedly. Just ahead of you the patch of brilliance from your headlights slips over the road and melts into mysterious shadows beyond. A vanishing tail light leads you on, and first thing you know you have wandered far afield.

Minutes slip into hours as the miles speed by. When you wind and set your faithful Westclox just before you keep your tardy date with your pillow, you are grateful to the timepiece to whom you trust your sleeping hours.

You may not feel so friendly toward it in the morning, but right now you can thank it in advance for the restful, unworried sleep that your confidence in Westclox makes possible. The trade mark Westclox is on the dial of every one to show our pride in it.

WESTERN CLOCK COMPANY, LA SALLE, ILLINOIS, U. S. A.

Factory: Peru, Illinois. *In Canada:* Western Clock Co., Limited, Peterborough, Ont.

Westclox *Big Ben* 7 inches tall. 4½-inch dial. Runs 32 hours. Steady and intermittent alarm, $3.25. In Canada, $4.50.

Westclox *Baby Ben* 3¾ inches tall. 2¾-inch dial. Runs 32 hours. Steady and intermittent alarm, $3.25. In Can., $4.50.

Westclox *America* 6¼ inches tall. 4-inch dial. Nickel case. Runs 32 hours. Top bell alarm, $1.50. In Canada, $2.00.

Westclox *Jack o'Lantern* 5 inches tall. Luminous dial and hands. Back bell alarm. Runs 32 hours, $3.00. In Canada, $4.00.

Westclox *Sleep-Meter* 5 inches tall. Nickeled case. 4-inch dial. Back bell alarm. Runs 32 hours, $2.00. In Canada, $3.00.

Westclox *Pocket Ben* A nickel plated watch. Stem wind and set. Neat hands and dial. Dependable, $1.50. In Canada, $2.00.

Westclox *Glo-Ben* Nickel-plated watch. Stem wind and set. Black face, luminous dial and hands, $2.25 In Canada, $3.50.

Westclox

That on-time feeling

THERE'S a sense of accomplishment in getting your feet on the floor about the second tap of the bell of your Westclox punctual call.

It gives you time to dress and breakfast leisurely. The trip to work is a satisfaction when you can take it easy. You walk into office or shop with a clear conscience, ready to start your work on time to the tick.

Things seem to go better on mornings when you start right. You give the boss value received or better, and have the feeling that if anyone in your department is due for a fatter pay envelope you have a fair chance for it.

Your Westclox is ready and willing. It will sound its call punctually at whatever time you set.

It is easy to choose a punctual, dependable alarm. Look for the trade mark Westclox on the dial and six cornered, orange-bordered buff tag.

WESTERN CLOCK COMPANY, LA SALLE, ILLINOIS, U. S. A.

Factory: Peru, Illinois. *In Canada:* Western Clock Co., Limited, Peterborough Ont.

Westclox *Big Ben* 7 inches tall. 4½-inch dial. Runs 32 hours. Steady and intermittent alarm. $3.50. In Canada, $4.50.

Westclox *Baby Ben* 3¼ inches tall. 2½-inch dial. Runs 32 hours. Steady and intermittent alarm, $3.50. In Can., $4.50.

Westclox *America* 6¼ inches tall. 4-inch dial. Nickel case. Runs 32 hours. Top-bell alarm, $1.50. In Canada, $2.00.

Westclox *Jack o'Lantern* 5 inches tall. Luminous dial and hands. Backbellalarm. Runs 32 hours, $3.00. In Canada, $4.00.

Westclox *Sleep-Meter* 5 inches tall. Nickeled case. 4-inch dial. Back bell alarm. Runs 32 hours, $2.00. In Canada, $3.00.

Westclox *Pocket Ben* A nickel plated watch. Stem wind and set. Neat hands and dial. Dependable, $1.50. In Canada, $2.00.

Westclox *Glo-Ben* Nickel-plated watch. Stem wind and set. Black face, luminous dial and hands, $2.50. In Canada, $3.50.

Westclox

Vacation Time

BABY BEN rides in the traveling bags of salesmen, actors and chautauqua entertainers to whom punctual calls at unusual hours are important.

These people must make the most of the sleep they can snatch, so they put Baby Ben on the job and rest easy. Baby Ben is sure to be awake to call at two or at six.

In strange rooms, the glowing dial of Baby Ben Luminous is convenient.

If you plan a summer outing in which early morning trips are part of the program, you can find a place for Baby Ben in your luggage, no matter how lightly you travel. For your pocket, Pocket Ben, a sturdy watch, or Glo-Ben, a watch that shows time in the dark.

Careful buyers always look for the trade mark Westclox on the dial.

WESTERN CLOCK COMPANY, LA SALLE, ILLINOIS, U. S. A.

Factory: Peru, Illinois. *In Canada:* Western Clock Co., Limited, Peterborough, Ont.

Westclox *Big Ben* 7 inches tall. 4½-inch dial. Runs 32 hours. Steady and intermittent alarm, $3.50. In Canada, $4.50.

Westclox *Baby Ben* 3¼ inches tall. 2½-inch dial. Runs 32 hours. Steady and intermittent alarm, $3.50. In Can., $4.50.

Westclox *America* 6¼ inches tall, 4-inch dial. Nickel case. Runs 32 hours. Top-bell alarm, $1.50. In Canada, $2.00.

Westclox *Jack o'Lantern* 5 inches tall. Luminous dial and hands. Back bellalarm. Runs 32 hours, $3.00. In Canada, $4.00.

Westclox *Sleep-Meter* 5 inches tall. Nickeled case. 4-inch dial. Back bell alarm. Runs 32 hours, $2.00. In Canada, $3.00.

Westclox *Pocket Ben* A nickelplatedwatch. Stem wind and set. Neat hands and dial. Dependable, $1.50. In Canada, $2.00.

Westclox *Glo-Ben* Nickel-plated watch. Stem wind and set. Black face, luminous dial and hands, $2.50. In Canada, $3.00.

Westclox

Luminous dials for long nights

WHEN fourteen hours of the twenty-four are so dark they all look the same, it is easy to sleep past your rising hour. Any Westclox alarm will call you on the dot.

You might wake at midnight, or at five-thirty. Then a Westclox luminous dial shows the time. A circle of numerals and two pointers glowing against the dark show the hour. And you sink comfortably back to sleep to wait your call.

Westclox luminous dials add a dollar or more to the cost—the radium luminous material is precious, and must be applied by hand. The doubled usefulness offsets the difference in price.

Big Ben Luminous $4.75, in Canada $6.00. Baby Ben Luminous, $4.75, in Canada $6.00. Glo-Ben $2.50, in Canada $3.50. All with the trade mark Westclox on the dial and six cornered, orange-bordered tag.

WESTERN CLOCK CO., LA SALLE, ILLINOIS, U. S. A.
Factory: Peru, Illinois. *In Canada:* Western Clock Co., Limited, Peterborough, Ont.

Westclox *Big Ben* 7 inches tall. 4½-inch dial. Runs 32 hours. Steady and intermittent alarm, $3.50. In Canada, $4.50.

Westclox *Baby Ben* 3¾ inches tall. 2¾-inch dial. Runs 32 hours. Steady and intermittent alarm, $3.50. In Canada, $4.50.

Westclox *America* 6¾ inches tall. 4-inch dial. Nickel case. Runs 32 hours. Top bell alarm, $1.50. In Canada, $2.00.

Westclox *Jack o'Lantern* 5 inches tall. Luminous dial and hands. Back bell alarm. Runs 32 hours, $3.00. In Canada, $4.00.

Westclox *Sleep-Meter* 5 inches tall. Nickeled case. 4-inch dial. Back bell alarm. Runs 32 hours, $2.00. In Canada, $3.00.

Westclox *Pocket Ben* A nickel plated watch. Stem wind and set. Neat hands and dial. Dependable, $1.50. In Canada, $2.00.

Westclox *Glo-Ben* Nickel plated watch. Stem wind and set. Black face, luminous dial and hands, $2.50. In Canada, $3.50.

Pocket Ben
$1.50

America
$1.50

Select any Westclox with confidence

THE America alarm and the Pocket Ben watch, both at $1.50, are fine examples of Westclox value. They're both dependable—built for long, satisfactory service, just like all time-pieces that wear the well-known Westclox trade-mark.

You can select any Westclox with confidence—for the same precision standards that make Big Ben dependable are applied to all the lower priced models.

You'll find the attractive new Auto Clock mighty convenient and practical for your car. It's a reliable Westclox, too.

Westclox prices range from $1.50 to $3.75. Same models with luminous night-and-day dials—$2.25 to $5.00.

Baby Ben De Luxe $3.75

Big Ben De Luxe $3.75

Ben Hur $2.50

New Auto Clock $2.50
Quickly attached on dash or above windshield. Fits any car

Baby Ben $3.25

Big Ben $3.25

Sleep-Meter $2.00

Sold everywhere by jewelers, druggists, hardware and department stores. Prices slightly higher in Canada

WESTERN CLOCK COMPANY, LA SALLE, ILLINOIS, U. S. A.
Factory: Peru, Ill. *In Canada:* Western Clock Company, Limited, Peterborough, Ont.

Westclox

—that's Big Ben's family name

The face in the dark

IN the middle of the night you ease up in your sleep; you wonder how long you have left. You aim one eye at your luminous Westclox, and there is the time.

Painted in soft light against the blackness are the numbers and hands that tell you the hour; designed to loom clearly out of the dark, and coated with a radium compound that will last for years.

For the man who likes a good-looking timepiece that realizes its responsibility, that will call him punctually, and will tell him the time at night as quickly as in broad daylight—Big Ben Luminous, \$5.00.

For the man or woman who needs a small clock that is easily carried about, that rings punctually and gently, that steadily glows the hour to save groping for a light—Baby Ben Luminous, \$5.00.

For the man or boy who wants a dependable timepiece for the pocket, Pocket Ben with plain dial, \$2.00; Glo-Ben for night and day time-telling, \$3.25.

The trade mark Westclox is on the six-sided, orange-bordered tag and on the dial of each timepiece.

WESTERN CLOCK CO., LA SALLE, ILLINOIS, U. S. A.

Makers of *Westclox:* Big Ben, Baby Ben, Pocket Ben, Glo-Ben, America, Sleep-Meter, Jack o'Lantern

Factory: Peru, Illinois. *In Canada:* Western Clock Co., Limited, Peterborough, Ont.

Useful gifts are best— A Westclox will be appreciated

Baby Ben \$3.25 *Big Ben Luminous \$4.50 also Plain \$3.25* *Baby Ben Luminous \$4.50*

YOUR friends will welcome Westclox as Christmas gifts, because they are useful and dependable.

There's a place in every home for another Westclox; and there's many a man or boy who will be glad to have a Westclox watch.

A variety of models, varying in design and price, but uniform in quality. The name "Westclox" on the dial is your protection. Luminous dials from \$2.25 to \$4.50. Plain dials from \$1.50 to \$3.25. Prices slightly higher in Canada.

WESTERN CLOCK CO., LA SALLE, ILLINOIS, U. S. A.

Factory: Peru, Illinois. *In Canada:* Western Clock Co., Limited, Peterborough, Ont.

A Merry Christmas from the whole Westclox family

THE SATURDAY EVENING POST
Westclox
Pocket Ben
To start the new year
WHEN you are sound asleep it is hard to remember your New Year's resolution to be on time mornings.
A Westclox alarm will keep it in mind and call you punctually at whatever time you want to get up.
Use your resolution on these dark mornings to rise promptly at the call of your Westclox.
You will find an assortment of Westclox alarms in plain and luminous dials in various sizes, styles and prices. Every one must prove its ability to run on time, ring on time, stay on time, before it is allowed to wear the trade mark Westclox on its dial and six-cornered, orange bordered, buff tag.
For time to and from home, and in between, a Westclox watch in your pocket will match time with the home clock.
WESTERN CLOCK CO., LA SALLE, ILLINOIS, U. S. A.
Factory: Peru, Illinois. In Canada: Western Clock Co., Limited, Peterborough, Ont
Westclox Big Ben 7 inches tall. 4½-inch dial. Runs 32 hours. Steady and intermittent alarm, $3.50. In Canada, $4.50.
Westclox Baby Ben 3¾ inches tall. 2½-inch dial. Runs 32 hours. Steady and intermittent alarm, $3.50. In Canada, $4.50.
Westclox America 6¾ inches tall. 4-inch dial. Nickel case. Runs 32 hours. Top bell alarm, $1.50. In Canada, $2.00.
Westclox Jack o' Lantern 5 inches tall. Luminous dial and hands. Back bell alarm. Runs 32 hours, $3.00. In Canada, $4.00.
Westclox Sleep-Meter 5 inches tall. Nickeled case. 4-inch dial. Back bell alarm. Runs 32 hours, $2.00. In Canada, $3.00.
Westclox Pocket Ben A nickel plated watch. Stem wind and set. Neat hands and dial. Dependable $1.50. In Canada, $2.00.
Westclox Glo-Ben Nickel plated watch. Stem wind and set. Black face, luminous dial and hands, $2.50. In Canada, $3.50.

Westclox
Pocket Ben
The Care of Your Westclox Watch
When business calls
MANY a sho… hing … n stretches way past b… e. The drone of the motor, a perfect … the rushing into the darkness beyond … headlights, the sense of exploration carries us too far afield.
But days were made for work and, much as we'd like to sleep through, the rising hour comes at the same old time and your Westclox will be punctually on the job.
So sleep easily, unworried, confident that your faithful timekeeper will rouse you on the dot.
Before any Westclox is allowed to carry that name on its dial, or wear its orange-bordered, six-sided buff tag, it must prove its ability to run on time, ring on time, stay on time.
To keep time in your pocket while you are away from the house—Pocket Ben, a sturdy Westclox watch that will give you good satisfaction at a price that is reasonable.
To be sure of getting a Westclox, look for the name on the dial and tag.
WESTERN CLOCK CO., LA SALLE, ILLINOIS, U. S. A.
Factory: Peru, Illinois. In Canada: Western Clock Co., Limited, Peterborough, Ont.
Westclox Big Ben 7 inches tall. 4½-inch dial. Runs 32 hours. Steady and intermittent alarm, $3.50. In Canada, $4.50.
Westclox Baby Ben 3¾ inches tall. 2½-inch dial. Runs 32 hours. Steady and intermittent alarm, $3.50. In Canada, $4.50.
Westclox Jack o' Lantern 5 inches tall. Luminous dial and hands. Back bell alarm. Runs 32 hours, $3.00. In Canada, $4.00.
Westclox Sleep-Meter 5 inches tall. Nickeled case. 4-inch dial. Back bell alarm. Runs 32 hours, $2.00. In Canada, $3.00.
Westclox Glo-Ben Nickel plated watch. Stem wind and set. Black face, luminous dial and hands, $2.50 In Canada, $3.50.

JANNEY, SEMPLE, HILL & CO.

2076 WATCHES AND CLOCKS

WATCHES

Ingersoll.

This is the jeweled Waterbury with the same movement as the ordinary Waterbury and the additional "tell the time in the dark" feature. For those who want a stylish, good-looking and good time-keeping watch with the Radiolite dial this is an ideal timepiece.

Waterbury Radiolite Black—Solid nickel [illegible] h a four-jewel movement; [illegible] inous hands and numerals. [illegible] $5.50

[illegible] n exceptionally handsome model. It is [illegible] with a Radiolite, but instead of being [illegible] the [illegible] tell the time in the dark" effect is se- [illegible] by means of a beautiful silver background.

[illegible] y Radiolite Silver—Solid nickel case, fitted with a four-jewel movement. Silver dial, luminous hands and numerals. Each $5.00

Waterbury Radiolite Gold—Gold case, otherwise same as nickel case. Each $8.00

Pocket Ben.

Pocket Ben is neat, well designed and finely finished. The dial is clear and distinct. Westclox movement guaranteed for one year. Each dozen is packed in carton with two display cards for windows or show case.

Pocket Ben—Stem wind and stem set. Shipping weight, per dozen, 9 pounds. Each $1.50

Glo Ben — Luminous dial, otherwise same as Pocket Ben. Each $2.25

One in a box.

ALARM CLOCKS

Victory.

8-day movement; brass case, heavily nickel plated; drop ring handle; sturdy legs; large dial; plain Arabic numerals which are easily read. Back bell alarm which is regulated by the ball on the top of the stem.

Victory—Nickel finish; ht., overall 7 inches; diameter, 3 inches; 4½ inch dial; weight, each, 2 pounds. Each $5.50

One in a carton.

ALARM CLOCKS

Big Ben.

Big Ben is out with another alarm clock improvement—dust-guards at every case-opening to protect the movement from dust and dirt. It stands 7 inches tall. Has a 4½ inch Arabic dial, on which the word Westclox appears. It calls steadily for five minutes, or intermittently at half-minute intervals for ten, on a deep-toned gong. The case is of brass, richly nickel plated. The winding keys are large and comfortable. The movement keeps excellent time and runs for 36 hours on one winding. Big Ben is six times factory tested.

Big Ben—Weight, each, 2¼ pounds. Each.....

Big Ben Luminous.

There is more to [illegible] luminous dials than me[illegible] coating numerals with r[illegible] um compound. The s[illegible] shape and spacing of [illegible] numerals make a great di[illegible]ference in the legibility [illegible] luminous dials. One set [illegible] hands makes time telling [illegible] night a simple matter, a[illegible] other set may prove confu[illegible]ing. The dial on Big Ben Luminous is good looking, day or night. The numerals are coated with a radium compound that holds its glow for years. The hands are broad and distinctive. The rest of the clock is Big Ben.

Big Ben Luminous—Weight, each, 2¼ lbs. Each..$4.50

Packed twelve in a carton.

Blue Bird.

Blue Bird sets a new standard for a top bell alarm. A novel, artistic top ring whose outline blends smoothly into that of the unusual, double dome bell; a highly polished, drawn brass case whose front rounds gracefully to hold the glass, legs that form a part of the attractive case outline, a dial whose clear-cut numerals of rugged character represent an advance in arrangement and legibility, and well designed hands. The word "Westclox" is on the face of this new timepiece. Blue Bird runs thirty hours with one winding, is thoroughly time tested, and rings at the hour set; a shut-off switch acts quickly.

Blue Bird—Weight, each, 1 lb. Each.....$1.75

Packed one in an individual box, 48 in a case.

All Right Hackett. 6" tall; 3-7/8" white dial. Intermittent alarm, shut off on back, top. Pat'd Oct. 28, 1902 through Sept. 23, 1913. Manufactured 8-9-1916. Value: $125

Alternating. 6-7/8" tall; 3-1/2" white dial. One piece case, brass ring, legs, and shut off lever. Pat'd Dec. 15, 1908. Mfg'd 3-25-1912. Value: $150

America. 6-1/4" tall; 3-1/4" white dial. One piece case, piecrust bezel, brass ring, legs, and shut off lever. Nice Western Clock Co. Trademark. Pat'd Oct. 28, 1902. Mfg'd 1-16-1907. Value: $175

America. 6-1/4" tall; 3-1/4" white dial. One piece case, piecrust bezel, brass ring, legs, and shut off lever. Pat'd Dec. 15, 1908. Mfg'd 10-22-1915. Value: $150

America. 6-1/4" tall; 3-1/4" white dial. One piece case, piecrust bezel. Pat'd Dec. 15, 1908. Mfg'd 6-12-1917. Value: $150

America. 6-1/4" tall; 3-1/4" white dial. Pat'd Dec. 15, 1908. Mfg'd 9-29-1923. Value: $125

America—One day, 4-inch dial, nickel plated case, alarm dial in front, sunk nickel plated back. Weight, each, 1 lb. Each....$1.50

America. 6-1/4" tall; 3-1/4" white dial. Shut off knob top right. Pat'd Dec. 1, 1925. Mfg'd 8-25-1929. Value: $125

America. 6-1/4" tall; 3-1/4" gold paper dial. Green painted case, shut off knob top right. Made in Petersborough, Canada. Mfg'd 5-1930. Value: $110

America. 6-1/4" tall; 3-1/4" black dial. Shut off knob top right, luminous numbers and hands. Pat'd Dec. 1, 1925. Mfg'd 2-25-1930. Value: $150

America. 5-1/2" tall; 3-1/2" white dial. Convex glass. Mfg'd 12-1932. Value: $90

Baby Ben. Private label dial. A.G. Tellner Jeweler and Optician Jamestown, No. Dak. 2-1/8" white dial; 4" tall. Pat'd Oct. 28, 1902 through Aug. 29, 1911. Mfg'd 3-13-1916. Value: $175

Baby Ben. 4" tall; 2-1/8" white dial. Pat'd Aug. 29, 1911. Mfg'd 11-24-1914. Value: $100

Baby Ben. 4" tall; 2-1/8" black dial. Luminous numbers and hands. Pat'd Aug. 29, 1911. Mfg'd 4-10-1919. Scratched on back: 9-13-1919 (Date Sold?) Value: $125

Baby Ben. 4" tall; 2-1/8" white dial. Pat'd Aug. 29, 1911. Mfg'd 4-10-1922. Value: $100

Genuine Baby Ben

Smallest member of the well-known Westclox family, but as accurate as their other one-day alarm Clocks. Nickel-plated case, 4 inches high with 2⅜-inch dial. Steady and intermittent alarm. We pay postage.

46 G 1155— Plain dial..... $3.25

46 G 1156— Luminous dial.. 4.50

Baby Ben. 4" tall; 2-1/8" white dial. Pat'd Nov. 9, 1920. Mfg'd 4-14-1924. Value: $100

Baby Ben. 4" tall; 2-1/8" black dial. Luminous numbers and hands. Made in Petersborough, Canada. Pat. Pending U.S.A. Mfg'd 6-1930. Value: $125

Big Ben. 7" tall; 4" white dial. Pat'd Oct. 28, 1902 through June 9, 1908. Oldest Big Ben known. Value: $250

Bantam. 4-3/4" tall; 3-1/4" white dial. Green painted case. Pat. Pend. U.S.A. Mfg'd 6-1931. Value: $90

Big Ben. Private label dial. Walter R. Blakely Jeweler and Optician Grafton, N.D. 7" tall; 4" white dial. Pat's infringed if resold under $2.50. Pat'd Oct. 28, 1902 through Aug. 29, 1911. Mfg'd 9-14-1912. Value: $190

Big Ben. 7" tall; 4" white dial. Pat'd April 15, 1919. Mfg'd 1-28-1925. Value: $125

Big Ben. 7" tall; 4" black dial. Luminous numbers and hands. Pat'd April 15, 1919. Mfg'd 6-17-1924. Value: $150

Big Ben. 7" tall; 4" white dial. Pat'd April 15, 1919. Mfg'd 2-20-1922. Value: $125

The Well Known Big Ben

Genuine "Big Ben," famous Westclox make—most popular of all nationally advertised One-Day alarm clocks. Has fully nickel-plated, dust-proof case 7 inches high, with 4⅜-inch dial. Steady and repeat alarm can be set at any time you wish. Best quality movement. We pay postage.

46 G 1151—Plain dial **$3.25**
46 G 1152—Luminous dial............. **4.50**

Big Ben. 7" tall; 4" white dial. Patents Pend. Mfg'd 3-1931. Value: $125

Private label Dial "C" Inside Double Diamond. 7" tall; 4" white dial. Pat'd Oct. 28, 1902 through Feb. 10, 1914. Value: $150

Big Ben. (Manufactured by Westclox) 4" paper dial; 7" nickel-plated case. Patents Oct. 28, 1902 through Feb. 10, 1914. Mfg'd 6-16-1915. Value: $125

Big Ben. Private label dial. W.W. Hazelton Jeweler Calmar, Iowa. 7" tall; 4" white dial. Pat'd Oct. 28, 1902 through Feb. 10, 1914. Value: $175

Big Ben. Private label dial. D.L. Hoefle Jeweler Newell, Iowa. 7" tall; 4" white dial. Pat'd Oct. 28, 1902 through Feb. 10, 1914. Mfg'd 10-29-1914. Value: $175

Big Ben. Private label dial. F.D. Gibbs Jeweler Sanborn, Iowa. 7" tall; 4" white dial. Pat'd Oct. 28, 1902 through April 15, 1919. Mfg'd 9-6-1924. Value: $175

Big Ben. Private label dial. W.M. James Jeweler Breckenridge, Minn. 7" tall; 4" white dial. Pat'd Oct. 28, 1902 through Aug. 29, 1911. Mfg'd 10-13-1913. Scratched on back: 10-23-16. Value: $175

Big Ben. Private label dial. John Dwyer Jeweler Chisholm, Minn. 7" tall; 4" white dial. Pat'd Oct. 28, 1902 through Feb. 10, 1914. Mfg'd 5-20-1915. Value: $175

Big Ben. Private label dial. C.D. Liedal Jeweler and Optometrist Fergus Falls, Minn. 7" tall; 4" white dial. Pat'd Oct. 28, 1902 through Feb. 10, 1914. Mfg'd 7-9-1918. Value: $175

Big Ben. Private label dial. F.H. Straub Optometrist and Jeweler Fergus Falls, Minn. 7" tall; 4" white dial. Pat'd May 24, 1910 through Dec. 1, 1925. Mfg'd 10-15-1926. Value: $175

Big Ben. Private label dial. B. Gerber Jeweler and Optician Frazee, Minn. Pat'd Oct. 28, 1902 through Feb. 10, 1914. Mfg'd 10-21-1914. 7" tall; 4" white dial. Value: $175

Big Ben. Private label dial. O.H. Olson Jeweler Paynesville, Minnesota. 7" tall; 4" white dial. Pat'd Oct. 28, 1902 through Feb. 10, 1914. Mfg'd 10-22-1914. Value: $175

Big Ben. Private label dial. P.E. Johnson Jeweler and Optician Abercrombie, N.D. 7" tall; 4" white dial. Pat'd Oct. 28, 1902 through Aug. 29, 1911. Mfg'd 3-14-1914. Value: $175

Big Ben. Private label dial. Carl W. Slocum Jeweler Cando, N.D. 7" tall; 4" white dial. Pat'd Oct. 28, 1902 through Feb. 10, 1914. Mfg'd 5-17-1918. Value: $175

Big Ben. Private label dial. R.E. Kreader Jeweler Cogswell, N.D. 7" tall; 4" white dial. Pat'd Oct. 28, 1902 through Feb. 10, 1914. Value: $175

Big Ben. Private label dial. Hagen-Newton Co. Jewelers Fargo, N.D. 7" tall; 4" white dial. Pat'd Oct. 28, 1902 through Feb. 10, 1914. Scratched on back: 10-10-19. Value: $175

Big Ben. Private label dial. Chas. A. Frost Jeweler Lisbon, No. Dak. 7" tall; 4" white dial. Pat'd Oct. 28, 1902 through Feb. 10, 1914. Mfg'd 1-31-1918. Value: $175

Big Ben. Private label dial. Lloyd A. Morrison Jeweler Valley City, N.D. 7" tall; 4" white dial. Pat'd Oct. 28, 1902 through Aug. 29, 1911. Mfg'd 8-8-1914. Value: $175

Big Ben. Private label dial. W.N. Matthews Alexandria, S.D. 7" tall; 4" white dial. Pat'd Oct. 28, 1902 through Feb. 10, 1914. Mfg'd 2-26-1926. Value: $175

Big Ben. Private label dial. Edwin J. Milberg Watchmaker, Jeweler, and Engraver Colville, Wash. 7" tall; 4" white dial. Pat'd Oct. 28, 1902 through Feb. 10, 1914. Mfg'd 10-16-1913. Value: $175

Big Ben. Private label dial. Stone-Fisher Co. Tacoma, Wash. 7" tall; 4" white dial. Pat'd Oct. 28, 1902 through Feb. 10, 1914. Mfg'd 8-7-1919. Value: $175

Big Ben. Private label dial. J.W. Wightman Elroy, Wisc. 7" tall; 4" white dial. Pat'd Oct. 28, 1902 through Aug. 29, 1911. Mfg'd 4-25-1914. Value: $175

Bingo. 6-1/2" tall; 3-3/4" white dial. Pat'd Dec. 15, 1908. Mfg'd 6-25-1919. Value: $125

Black Bird. 6" tall; 3-1/4" black dial. Luminous numbers and hands. Pat'd Dec. 1, 1925. Mfg'd 8-10-1926. Scratched on back: 9-10-1926. Value: $150

Black Bird.

A Westclox that offers good looks, a high grade luminous dial at a low price. It stands six inches tall, has a double dome top bell, drawn brass case, heavily nickeled, 30-hour Westclox movement. 3½-inch black Arabic dial, with needle-fine polished steel pivots, rust-proof hairspring, numerals and hands coated with radium compound. They will glow for years. Steady alarm with handle shut-off attachment.

Black Bird—Weight, each, 1 pound. Each **$2.50**

Blue Bird. 5-7/8" tall; 3-1/4" white dial. Pat'd Oct. 28, 1902 through Dec. 15, 1908. Mfg'd 11-2-1921. Value: $125

Blue Bird. 6" tall; 3-1/4" white dial. Dark blue painted case. Pat'd Dec. 1, 1925. Mfg'd 1928. Value: $125

Blue Bird. 6-1/4" tall; 3-1/4" white dial. Patent Pending. Mfg'd 3-1931. Value: $125

Bull's Eye. 6-3/4" tall; 3-1/2" white dial. One piece case, piecrust bezel. Pat'd Dec. 15, 1908. Mfg'd 3-25-1912. Value: $175

Bunkie. 6" tall; 3-3/4" white dial. Pat'd Oct. 29, 1902 through Sept. 23, 1913. Mfg'd 8-15-1921. Value: $150

Eclipse. 6-1/4" tall; 3-1/4" white dial. Brass ring and legs, one piece case. Pat'd Sept. 22, 1885. Mfg'd 2-21-1908. Value: $150

Eclipse. 6-1/4" tall; 3-1/4" white dial. Brass legs and ring. Pat'd Oct. 26, 1902. Value: $150

Good Morning. 6" tall; 3-1/4" white dial. Pat'd Oct. 28, 1902 through Dec. 15, 1908. Mfg'd 11-3-1924. Value: $125

Good Morning. 5-1/2" tall; 3-1/4" white dial. Made in Canada. Mfg'd 1932. Value: $90

Jack O' Lantern. 6" tall; 3-1/4" black dial. Luminous numbers and hands, narrow bezel. Pat'd Oct. 28, 1902 through Dec. 15, 1908. Value: $150

Sleep-Meter and Jack O'Lantern

Another One-Day alarm Clock member of the Westclox family. Nickel-plated; 3½-inch dial. Height, 5¼ inches. We pay postage.

46 G 1157— Sleep-Meter, plain dial. **$2.00**

46 G 1158— Jack O'Lantern, luminous dial.... **$3.00**

Jack O' Lantern. 5-1/2" tall; 3-1/4" black dial. Luminous numbers and hands. Pat. Sept. 23, 1913. Mfg'd 10-28-1925. Value: $125

Jack O' Lantern. 5-1/2" tall; 3-1/4" black dial. Luminous numbers and hands. Pat. Sept. 23, 1913. Mfg'd 2-14-1918. Value: $125

Jack O' Lantern. 5-1/2" tall; 3-1/4" black dial. Luminous numbers and hands. Pat. Dec. 1, 1925. Mfg'd 8-19-1926. Value: $125

WESTCLOX

Jack o'Lantern.

Jack o'Lantern—Weight, each, 1½ lbs. Each....$3.00
Packed 12 in a carton, 48 in a case.

Keno. 4-1/2" tall; 3-1/4" white dial. Green painted case, patent pending. Mfg'd 11-1931. Value: $90

La Sallita. 3-1/8" tall; 1-3/4" white dial. Brass ring and legs, piecrust bezel, beveled glass. Pat. Dec. 15, 1908. Mfg'd 5-6-1918. Value: $110

Lookout. 6-1/4" tall; 2-1/4" white dial. Brass case. Pat'd Dec. 15, 1908. Mfg'd 6-12-1917. Value: $135

Lookout. 6-1/4" tall; 2-1/4" white dial. Pat'd Dec. 15, 1908. Mfg'd 6-14-1921. Value: $135

Lookout. 6-1/4" tall; 2-1/4" white dial. Pat'd Dec. 15, 1908. Mfg'd 11-30-1923. Value: $135

Monitor. 6" tall; 3-1/4" white dial. Brass legs and ring. Pat'd Dec. 1, 1925. Mfg'd 2-24-1928. Value: $125

Renown. 5-1/4" tall; 3-1/4" white dial. Scratched on back: 12/13/30. Value: $90

Silver Bell. 6-1/4" tall; 3-1/4" white dial. Case painted green, scratched on back: 10/6/42. Repair date? Value: $125

Sleep Meter. 5-1/2" tall; 3-1/4" white dial. Pat'd Sept. 23, 1913. Mfg'd 9-16-1918. Value: $110

Sleep Meter. 5-1/2" tall; 3-1/4" white dial. Pat'd Sept. 23, 1913. Mfg'd 11-20-1924. Value: $110

Sleep Meter. 5-1/2" tall; 3-1/4" white dial. Pat'd Sept. 23, 1913. Mfg'd 11-10-1925. Value: $110

Sleepmeter.

The sleepmeter is a 1-day movement with back bell alarm; it is five inches in height and four inches in diameter. The dial is particularly pleasing and legible. The alarm is long and loud and can be shut off at will by means of the shut-off attachment right above the bell. Weight, each, 1½ lbs. Each..$2.00

Put up in a strong box with an attractive colored label, and packed one dozen in a carton. Dealer's name printed free on dials in case lots of 48.

Sleep Meter. 5-1/2" tall; 3-1/4" black dial. Luminous numbers and hands. Pat'd Sept. 23, 1913. Mfg'd 3-31-1928. Value: $135

The Sphinx. Private label dial. Andrews Jewellers 276 Washington St. Cor Water St. Boston. 5" tall; 3-1/4" white dial. Piecrust bezel, pat'd Oct. 28, 1902 through Sept. 23, 1913. Mfg'd 8-12-1914. Value: $195

Walwoja. 6-1/4" tall; 3-1/4" white dial. Green painted case, pat'd Dec. 1, 1925. Mfg'd 1-25-1929. Value: $150

Westclox. 3-1/8" tall; 1-3/4" white celluloid dial. Piecrust bezel, beveled glass. Pat'd Dec. 15, 1908. Mfg'd 1-21-1916. Value: $110

Westclox. 3-1/4" tall; 1-3/4" white celluloid dial. Piecrust bezel, beveled glass, brass ring and legs. Pat'd Dec. 15, 1908. Mfg'd 1-21-1916. Value: $110

Westclox. 5-7/8" tall; 3-1/8" white dial. Piecrust bezel, brass legs, shut off, and ring. Nice old Western Clock Co. Trademark. Pat'd Oct. 28, 1902 through Dec. 15, 1908. Mfg'd 5-28-1910. Value: $175

Westclox. 6-1/4" tall; 3-1/4" white dial. Made in Canada. Mfg'd 12-1934. Value: $125

Westclox. 5-1/2" tall; 3-1/4" gold paper dial. Luminous numbers and hands. Made in Canada. Pat'd U.S.A. Mfg'd 10-1932. Value: $90

Westclox. Eastman Timer. Eastman Kodak Co. Rochester, N.Y. 5-3/4" tall; 3-3/8" white dial. Small 2" round 30 hour time only movement. No shut off, it just runs. Pat'd Sept. 2, 1902 through Feb. 2, 1909. Value: $100

Movement of Big Ben Alarm with mainspring barrel removed showing date of manufacture, 3-15-16.

Westclox. Honoring Spanish American War of 1898. 6-1/4" tall; 3-1/2" multi-colored dial. Brass ring and legs. Dial pat'd 9-12-99 by Regent Mfg. Co., Chicago. Dial showing President McKinley and the war heroes; Schlev, Sampson, Sigsbee, Evans, Clark, Funston, Wheeler, Otis, Shafter, Roosevelt, Miles, and Dewey. Pat'd June 4, 1907. Value: $550

Foreign

I consider a foreign clock to be any clock manufactured outside of the United States that I cannot attribute to an American manufacturer.

Made in Germany. 10" tall; 4-3/8" white dial with gold filigree design. Double-beaded brass design circle case, brass ring, legs, and alarm shut off lever. Seconds bit. Value: $175

Tapageur. Made in France. 5" tall; 2-3/4" metal silver dial. Luminous numbers and hands. Scratched on case: 4-29-44. Value: $90

T H. Made in Germany by Thomas Haller, Schwenninggen, Germany. 6" tall; 3-1/4" white dial. Seconds bit, brass ring, and shut off. Registered 29 Jan. 1896. Value: $125

Junghans. 3-1/4" paper dial; 7" nickel-plated case, with brass legs and top piece. Seconds bit. Earliest scratch mark on back: 2-25-1903. Value: $150

Blinking Eye. 3-1/4" colorful dial, animated blinking eyes when running; 6-1/4" nickel-plated case with brass legs and top piece. K.C. Co. Germany on bottom of dial. Made in Wurttemberg stamped into back of clock. Value: $650

Made in Germany. 1-5/8" paper dial; 3-1/4" white alabaster case, with brass legs and brass bezel. Value: $75

Thrill. 2-5/8" tall; 1-7/8" white dial. Luminous numbers and hands, red painted case. Swiss made. Value: $65

Unico. 2" tall; 1-1/16" silver metal dial. Luminous numbers and hands. Swiss made. Value: $55

Veglia. Made in Italy. 4-1/8" tall; 2-3/16" white dial. Alarm shut off top left, steady-repeat top right. Value: $65

Veglia. Made in Italy. 4-1/8" tall; 2-3/16" white dial. Alarm shut off top left, steady-repeat top right. Value: $65

Hamburg American Clock Co. 8-1/4" tall; 3-3/8" white dial. Celluloid dial with brass center, copper-plated brass case. Dial indicator on back of case for alarm set. Value: $195

Hamburg American Clock Co. 5-1/2" tall; 3-3/8" celluloid dial. Brass center, copper-plated brass case, brass ornaments and legs. Scratched on back: HP-1880. Value: $150

Made in Germany. 3-3/8" tall; 1-5/8" white dial. White celluloid dial with wine colored dots and silver numbers. Brass case. Value: $100

Made in Germany. 3-1/4" tall; 1-5/8" white dial. Maroon colored numbers, celluloid case. Value: $125

Made in Germany. 9-3/4" tall; 4-3/8" brass dial. Raised numeral spots and raised minute markers, brass legs. Value: $195

Made in Germany. 9-3/4" tall; 4-3/8" brass dial. Raised time track, brass alarm shut off lever, and legs. Value: $195

Made in Germany. 7-1/8" tall; 3-1/4" white dial. Dial tinted light green, brass legs, alarm shut off lever, and hammer. Seconds bit. Value: $175

Made in Germany. 6-1/4" tall; 3-1/4" white dial. Seconds bit, brass legs, alarm shut off lever, and hammer. Value: $150

Made in Germany. 6-5/8" tall; 3-1/4" white dial. Brass alarm shut off, seconds bit. Value: $125

6-1/8" tall; 3-1/2" white dial. Alarm shut off top left. Movement dated 8-26. Value: $95

Made in Germany. 3" tall; 1-7/8" brass dial. Beveled glass, brass case. Original wood case covered in black leatherette, with dark green velvet covering the inside. Value: $125

Marshall-Wells Hardware Co. 2765
Mar. 1, 1914

WIRELESS INTERMITTENT ALARM CLOCKS

We Guarantee this Clock to give Perfect Satisfaction and Keep Correct Time for a Period of Two Years; If it Fails to do this we will, upon its return to us, Transportation Charges Prepaid, Replace Same Free of Charge.

Cut Shows Full Size Clock

BABY WIRELESS

BABY WIRELESS

The Baby Wireless Alarm Clock is a New Creation—a Distinctive, Extra High Grade Clock, especially suited to the demand for a Dependable Alarm Clock.

The Finish is Distinctive and Exclusive; the Material throughout, both in the Works and the Case is the Best and the Two Year Guarantee Absolutely Assures Quality in every Detail of Construction.

Intermittent Light Sounding Alarm; Height 3½ in., Depth 2 in., White Dial 2 in. Diam.; Heavy Seamless Case, Assorted Finishes, Dust Proof, Plain Rim, Fancy Stationary Handle; Alarms Intermittently every 20 Seconds for 15 Minutes on 2 in. Metal Gong on Back; Shut-off Switch on Top; Easy Running and Long Wearing Escapement; Finely Tempered and Polished Spring.

	Each
No. 1C—Copper Finish	$2.00
No. 1GM—Gun Metal Finish	2.00
No. 1FB—French Bronze Finish	2.00
No. 1N—Nickel Plated Finish	2.00
No. 1B—Old Brass Finish	2.00
No. 1OC—Oxidized Copper Finish	2.00
No. 1S —Silver Finish	2.00

One in a Heavy Pasteboard Box; Weight ½ Lb. Each

50 in a Case; Weight 50 Lbs. per Case

BABY WIRELESS ASSORTMENTS

	Per Assortment
One Dozen Clocks, Complete with Hardwood Display Stand, 10½ in. High	$24.00

Weight 30 Lbs. per Assortment

Assorted as Follows:

	Retail Each
2 Only No. 1C—Copper Finish	$2.00
2 Only No. 1GM—Gun Metal Finish	2.00
2 Only No. 1FB—French Bronze Finish	2.00
2 Only No. 1N—Nickel Plated Finish	2.00
2 Only No. 1B—Old Brass Finish	2.00
2 Only No. 1OC—Oxidized Copper Fin.	2.00
1 Only —Display Stand Free	
Total Retail Value	$24.00

POPULAR ALARM CLOCK ASSORTMENT

This Rack Will Display Alarm Clocks so they will sell themselves

	Per Assortment
No. 101—Assortment Complete with Three Step Mission Display Stand; 13 in. High; See List below	$97.50

	Retail Price Each	Total Retail Value
1 Only No. 1C —Baby Wireless, Copper Finish	$2.00	$2.00
1 Only No. 1GM—Baby Wireless, Gun Metal Finish	2.00	2.00
1 Only No. 1FB—Baby Wireless, French Bronze Finish	2.00	2.00
1 Only No. 1N —Baby Wireless, Nickel Finish	2.00	2.00
1 Only No. 1B —Baby Wireless, Old Brass Finish	2.00	2.00
3 Only No. 2C —The Wireless, Copper Finish	2.00	6.00
3 Only No. 2GM—The Wireless, Gun Metal Finish	2.00	6.00
3 Only No. 2FB—The Wireless, French Bronze Finish	2.00	6.00
3 Only No. 2B —The Wireless, Old Brass Finish	2.00	6.00
3 Only No. 2OC—The Wireless, Oxidized Copper	2.00	6.00
2 Only No. 3C —Jumbo Wireless, Copper Finish	2.50	5.00
2 Only No. 3GM—Jumbo Wireless, Gun Metal Finish	2.50	5.00
2 Only No. 3FB—Jumbo Wireless, French Bronze Finish	2.50	5.00
2 Only No. 3B —Jumbo Wireless, Lemon Brass Finish	2.50	5.00
2 Only No. 3OC—Jumbo Wireless, Oxid. Copper Finish	2.50	5.00
5 Only No. 8M —Marathon 8 Day, Copper Finish	[illegible]	15.00
5 Only No. 95 —Wizard, Nickel Finish	1.50	7.50
10 Only No. 120 —Aerogram, Nickel Finish	1.00	10.00
Total		$97.50

2766 Marshall-Wells Hardware Co.
Feb. 1, 1914

WIRELESS INTERMITTENT ALARM CLOCKS

We Guarantee this Clock to give Perfect Satisfaction and Keep Correct Time for a Period of Two Years; If it Fails to do this, we will upon its return to us, Transportation Charges Prepaid, Replace Same Free of Charge.

THE WIRELESS

Cut Shows Full Size Clock

The Wireless Alarm Clock is a new creation—a distinctive, extra high grade Clock, especially suited to the demand for dependable Alarm Clocks.

The finish of these Clocks is distinctive and exclusive

They are not placed in competition with the common nickel finished, low grade alarms, and this makes it possible to retail these goods at a fair profit.

The material throughout is the best obtainable, and the two-year guarantee absolutely assures quality in every detail of construction.

Intermittent Alarm; Height 6¼ in., Depth 3¼ in.; 4½ in. White Dial; Heavy Seamless Case, Assorted Finishes, Dust Proof, Plain Rim; Fancy Stationary Handle; Alarms Intermittently every 20 seconds for 15 minutes on 4 in. Bell Metal Gong in Back; Shut-off Switch on top; Easy Running and Long Wearing Escapement; Finely Tempered and Polished Spring.

Dealer's Imprint (name and address) on the Dial Free of Charge in Case Lots of 50 Clocks, shipment at one time F. O. B. Factory.

	Each
[illegible]	$2.00
No. 2GM—Gun Metal Finish	2.00
No. 2F—French Bronze Finish	2.00
No. 2N—Nickel Finish	$2.00
No. 2B—Old Brass Finish	2.00
No. 2OC—Oxidized Copper	2.00
No. 2S—Silver Finish	2.00

Each Clock packed in a Box

Weight 1¼ Lbs. Each; Weight per Case (50 Clocks) 110 Lbs.

WIRELESS INTERMITTENT ALARM CLOCKS

e Guarantee this Clock to give Perfect Satisfaction and Keep Correct Time for a Period of Two Years; If it Fails to do this we will, upon its return to us, Transportation Charges Prepaid, Replace Same Free of Charge.

Easy to Read Dial

Loud Sounding Alarm

JUMBO WIRELESS

Cut Shows Full Size Clock

The Jumbo Wireless is the largest accurate time-keeping alarm clock on the market, the very latest development in one-day Time Intermittent Alarm Clocks, fitted with special hands, easy reading Roman time dial, Arabic Alarm Dial, beautiful top ornament, attractive design; seamless brass case, 4 inch bell metal gong on back. Rings intermittently every 20 seconds for 15 minutes. The alarm can be silenced by shut-off lever in upper left hand corner on the back of the clock. Can be furnished in the following beautiful finishes:

Copper, Gun Metal, French Bronze, Lemon Brass, Oxidized Copper

Height 8 inches; Width 6¼ inches; Dial 4¼ inches

Dealer's Imprint (name and address) on the Dial Free of Charge in Case Lots of 24 Clocks, Shipment at one time F. O. B. Factory

	Each		Each
No. 3C—Copper Finish	$2.50	No. 3F—French Bronze Finish	$2.50
No. 3GM—Gun Metal Finish	2.50	No. 3B—Lemon Brass Finish	2.50
No. 3S—Silver Finish	2.50	No. 3OC—Oxidized Copper Finish	2.50

Each Clock packed in a Box

Weight 2¼ Lbs. Each; Weight 85 Lbs. per Case (24 Clocks)

8-DAY MARATHON AUTOMATIC ALARM CLOCKS

The following directions are packed with each Clock. Read them carefully.

"Wind time and alarm side and be sure that switch on back of clock is turned toward the word "Alarm." Then turn the alarm indicator, or red hand, as arrow indicates on dial, until it is directly under the hour hand. If the Alarm does not ring the red hand may be turned to the hour at which alarm is desired to ring. It must be carefully observed that the red hand or indicator must pass by the hour hand once without the alarm ringing in order that the alarm will go off in twelve hours or less. Should it ring when indicator is passing the hour hand, push in on button marked "Stop Alarm" on back of clock and alarm will stop ringing. Then make another revolution of the dial with the red alarm hand and set at the hour you wish the clock to alarm. If a regular time for ringing alarm is desired there need be no further setting of indicator, as alarm will ring off every twenty-four hours.

To illustrate: The alarm is set at night to ring off at six o'clock in the morning. The alarm as expected rings at six o'clock in the morning. Now, if not further setting is done the following morning, or in twenty-four hours, the alarm will ring again and so on for seven days. If, however, you do not wish your alarm to ring on Sunday morning, or any other morning, all it is necessary to do is to throw the switch on back of clock to the word "silent."

But if you wish the alarm to ring at the regular time on Monday morning, before retiring Sunday night, press button and then throw switch on back of clock to the word "Alarm."

If these instructions are observed, you will have no trouble with the clock.

Wind it Once a Week

—

Guaranteed for Two Years

[8-DAY MARATHON AUTOMATIC

Cut Shows Full Size Clock

The 8-Day Marathon Automatic Alarm Clock is the latest creation in the manufacture of 20th Century Alarms. The 8-Day Marathon Modern Improved Movement with Automatic Alarm feature is the Zenith of Perfection known to the art of clock craftsmen. The noiseless beat (light tick) is especially desirable, and appeals strongly to the light sleeper. Only the highest grade of materials is used throughout the entire construction of the clock. It has all Steel Cut Pinions, with Extra Heavy Brass Plates and Wheels, which are not used by any other alarm clock maker at the present time. Has 4 in. Bell, Metal Gong on back, Arabic Dial, red alarm hand, fancy time hands, attractive top ornament. Brass seamless case, beautifully finished, in Copper, giving the clock a very attractive appearance, unlike that of the ordinary low priced alarm clocks.

Height 8 inches; Width 6¼ inches; Dial 4¼ inches

Dealer's Imprint (name and address) on dial, Free of Charge, in Case Lots of 24 Clocks, shipment at one time F. O. B. Factory.

	Each
No. 8C—Copper Finished	$3.00
No. 8B—Lemon Brass Finish	3.00
No. 8S—Silver Finish	3.00

Each Clock packed in Box; 24 Clocks Packed in Shipping Case; Weight Each 2¼ Lbs.; Weight Case of 24, 94 Lbs.

Marshall-Wells Hardware Co. 2768-1
Jan. 1, 1915

WIRELESS CALL ALARM CLOCKS

The Latest and Most Thoroughly Up-to-Date Alarm Clock, with many New Features not found in others of its type

It will Wake the Dairyman, the Farmer, the Train Man, the Mechanic, the Business Man and even the School Boy, who hates to get up at all.

One Day Time.
Alarm and Silent Switch.
Watch-Like Construction.
Dealer's Imprint on Dial when purchased in Case Lots.

Cut Shows Full Size Clock

Continuous or Intermittent Alarm

The Alarm which has a Clear, Silvery Note, sounds on a large Gong on the Back; While the tone is not harsh it is insistent, means business and will wake the most profound sleeper.

The Movement is made of Solid Brass, with highly polished Bearings of hard Pinion Steel; the Dial has large, plain Figures which are easily read even in a dim light.

Height 7⅛ in., Width 5¼ in.; Dial 4½ in.

Dealer's Imprint (Name and Address) on Dial, Free of Charge, in Case Lots of 24 Clocks, Shipment at One Time F. O. B. Factory

	Each
No. 5C —Copper Finish	$2.50
No. 5GM—Gun Metal Finish	2.50
No. 5F —French Bronze Finish	2.50
No. 5N —Nickel Finish	$2.50
No. 5B —Old Brass Finish	2.50
No. 5OC—Oxidized Copper Finish	2.50
No. 5S —Silver Finish	2.50

Each Clock Packed in a Box; 24 Clocks Packed in a Shipping Case; Weight 1¾ Lbs. Each; Weight of Case 86 Lbs.

For convenience, safety and economy in shipping, we advise the Dealer to buy these Clocks in Case Lots with his Name and Address on the Dial.

2768-2 Marshall-Wells Hardware Co.
Oct. 1, 1914

JUNIOR WIRELESS ALARM CLOCKS

INTERMITTENT ALARM; PORCELAIN DIAL

The Junior Wireless is one of the most pleasing Alarm Clocks of Medium Size that has ever been made; the Design is new and refined; the Porcelain Dial is plainly marked with large, clear Figures, which are easily read even in a dim light; the Alarm rings on large gong on the back of Clock and has a rich, musical tone which never fails to awaken the sleeper.

Height 5 in., Width 4 in.; 2½ in. Porcelain Dial; Fitted with "Alarm" or "Silent" Switch

	Each
No. 4B —Brass Finish	$2.50
No. 4C —Copper Finish	2.50
No. 4FB—French Bronze Finish	2.50
No. 4GM—Gun Metal Finish	2.50
No. 4N —Nickel Plated Finish	2.50
No. 4OC—Oxidized Copper Finish	2.50
No. 4S —Silver Finish	2.50

Weight 10 Oz. Each

24 in a Case; Weight 48 Lbs. per Case

EXCELLO ALARM CLOCKS

CONTINUOUS ALARM; PORCELAIN DIAL

The Excello is a "Smaller Brother" to the Junior Wireless and is identical in appearance, the only difference being in the Size and the Kind of Alarm; the Excello has a Continuous Alarm instead of an Intermittent Alarm. This Clock is bound to become very popular as it is High Grade in every respect and Moderate in Price.

Height 4¼ in., Width 3¼ in.; 2 in. Porcelain Dial; Fitted with "Alarm" or "Silent" Switch

	Each
No. 6B —Brass Finish	$2.00
No. 6C —Copper Finish	2.00
No. 6FB—French Bronze Finish	2.00
No. 6GM—Gun Metal Finish	2.00
No. 6N —Nickel Plated Finish	2.00
No. 6OC—Oxidized Copper Finish	2.00
No. 6S —Silver Finish	2.00

Weight 8 Oz. Each

24 in a Case; Weight 45 Lbs. per Case

2770 **Marshall-Wells Hardware Co.**
Nov. 1, 1913

CALL BOY ALARM CLOCKS

THE CLOCK WITH THE BELL INSIDE THE CASE

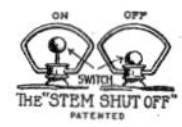

Front View

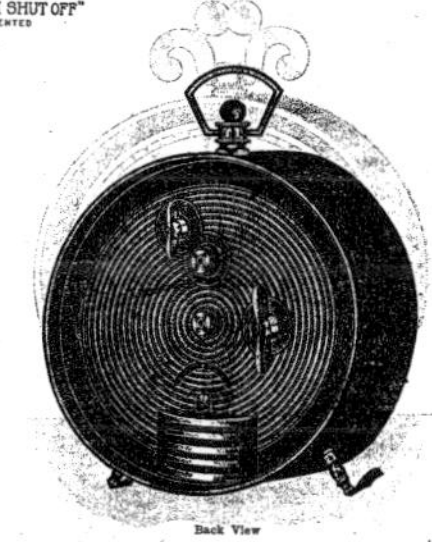

Back View

CALL BOY

One Day Alarm

A Low Priced Alarm Clock with the Bell Inside the Case and with Stem Shut Off; the Alarm is released by raising the Ball and is stopped by pressing Ball down

Each

Call Boy—Nickel Plated and Polished, Seamless Brass Case; Diameter 4½ in.; Height Over-all 5½ in.; Depth 2½ in.; Knurled Rim; White Dial; Each Clock Tested at Factory........ $2.50

One in a Box; Weight 1 Lb. Each

Old Style Nickel Alarm Clocks were made with the Bell on Top, not for beauty or serviceability, but because it appeared to be the most practicable and cheapest method of construction and the style has been continued for the same reason; owing, however, to the exposed position of the Bell it is always liable to displacement; this fact is universally recognized and is a source of constant annoyance. Furthermore, competition and general use have made the Clock with Bell on Top synonymous with cheapness.

THE "STEM SHUT OFF"

"The Call Boy Clock with the Bell Inside" and "Stem Shut Off" is without doubt the handsomest and most efficient low priced Alarm Clock ever made, and one you can make a profit on.

Marshall-Wells Hardware Co. 2769
Nov. 1, 1913

ALARM CLOCKS

We Guarantee these Clocks to give Satisfaction and Keep Correct Time for a period of One Year

WIZARD

Intermittent Alarm

Wizard Alarm Clocks are in every respect a high grade Clock and at moderate cost; they are accurate and dependable and embody in their construction and adjustment every detail for the making of a satisfactory Clock.

The Wizard meets the demand for high grade, nickel plated Clocks, at a popular price, and meets the competition of all nickel finished clocks of standard grade. Height 6¼ in., Depth 3¼ in.; 4½ in. White Dial; Seamless Brass Case, Full Nickel Plated; 4 in. Bell Metal Gong on Back; One Day Alarm, Rings Intermittently every 20 seconds for 10 minutes; Fitted with Silent Switch.

Dealer's Imprint (name and address) on the Dial Free of Charge in Case Lots of 50 Clocks, shipment at one time F. O. B. Factory.

Each

No. 95—Nickel Plated Finish........ $2.50

50 in a Case; Weight 110 Lbs. per Case
One in a Pasteboard Box; Weight 1¼ Lbs. Each

THE AEROGRAM

The Dust-Proof Seamless Case and 30 Hour Winding Features are found only in The Aerogram, which is Fully Guaranteed for One Year.

Height 6¼ in., Depth 2¾ in.; 4 in. White Dial; Dust-Proof Heavy Seamless Brass Case, Nickel Plated; Drop Handle; Switch for Stopping Alarm.

Dealer's Imprint (Name and Address) on Dial, Free of Charge, in Case Lots of 50 Clocks shipment at one time F. O. B. Factory.

Each

No. 120—Nickel Plated Finish........ $1.50

One in a Box; Weight 1¼ Lbs. Each
50 in a Case; Weight 80 Lbs. per Case

Every Merchant who is interested in advertising his business and building up his Trade should take advantage of every opportunity of keeping his name and business in the minds of his customers; we believe that having your name and business on these Clocks will prove a good means of stimulating trade not only on Clocks but on other lines as well.

Marshall-Wells Hardware Co. 2771
June 1, 1913

ALARM CLOCKS

Front View

Back View

EMPRESS EIGHT DAY LONG ALARM

Height 7¼ in.; the Movement is constructed with Cut Steel Pinions in the Time Train, same as a Watch; the Springs are encased in Barrels; in winding there is the same power on the Time Train as at any other time, which is not the case in Ordinary Alarm Clocks; the Empress has a large 5 in. Gong on the Back and the Shut-Off Switch on the Top is readable from the front; the 4½ in. Dial is Iveroid instead of paper as used in many Alarm Clocks; the Case is reinforced by a Steel Dust Cap; each Clock it Timed and Inspected before leaving the Factory; Fitted with Ring, Feet, Knob and Polished Brass Keys.

	Each
No. 90—Nickel Plated Finish	$2.50
No. 91—Brass Finish	2.50

Weight 1¾ Lbs. Each

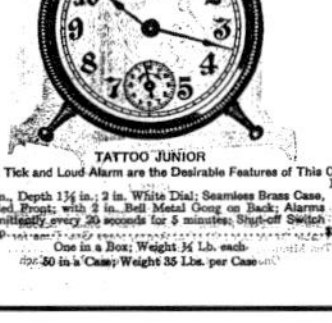

TATTOO JUNIOR

The Quiet Tick and Loud Alarm are the Desirable Features of This Clock

Each

Height 3 in., Depth 1¾ in.; 2 in. White Dial; Seamless Brass Case, Knurled Front; with 2 in. Bell Metal Gong on Back; Alarms Intermittently every 20 seconds for 5 minutes; Shut-off Switch at Top........ $2.00

One in a Box; Weight ¾ Lb. each
50 in a Case; Weight 35 Lbs. per Case

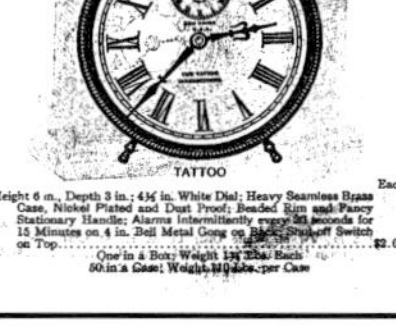

TATTOO

Each

Height 6 in., Depth 3 in.; 4½ in. White Dial; Heavy Seamless Brass Case, Nickel Plated and Dust Proof; Beaded Rim and Fancy Stationary Handle; Alarms Intermittently every 20 seconds for 15 Minutes on 4 in. Bell Metal Gong on Back; Shut-off Switch on Top........ $2.00

One in a Box; Weight 1¼ Lbs. Each
50 in a Case; Weight 110 Lbs. per Case

2772 — Marshall-Wells Hardware Co.

Nov. 1, 1913

ALARM CLOCKS

AMERICA
No Guarantee

	Each
Height 6¾ in., Depth 2¾ in.; 4 in. White Dial; Brass Case, Nickel Plated, with Beaded Rim; Folding Handle, with Shut-off	$1.00

One in a Box; Weight 1 Lb. Each
50 in a Case; Weight 78 Lbs. per Case

NEW RIVAL

	Each
Height 6¾ in., Depth 2¾ in.; 4 in. White Dial; Solid Pallet; Heavy Seamless Brass Case, Nickel Plated; New Style Beaded Rim; Drop Handle; Flush Back with Knurled Edges; All Trimmings are Heavily Nickel Plated; has Switch for Stopping Alarm	$1.50

One in a Box; Weight 1¼ Lbs. Each
50 in a Case; Weight 80 Lbs. per Case

FANCY ALARM CLOCKS

IRON CLAD
No Guarantee

	Each
Height 5 in., 3¼ in. White Dial; Bronze Plated Cast Iron Case; Rings 45 Seconds; can be Shut-off at will	$1.50

One in a Box; Weight 2¼ Lbs. Each

JOKER

	Each
Height 7 in., Width 5 in.; 3 in. White Dial; Gilt Front, Back and Handle; Nickel Plated Frame, Glass Sides; Second Hand; Visible Movement; Musical Alarm, plays One Tune for about Ten Minutes, instead of Ringing	$4.00

One in a Pasteboard Box; Weight 2 Lbs. Each

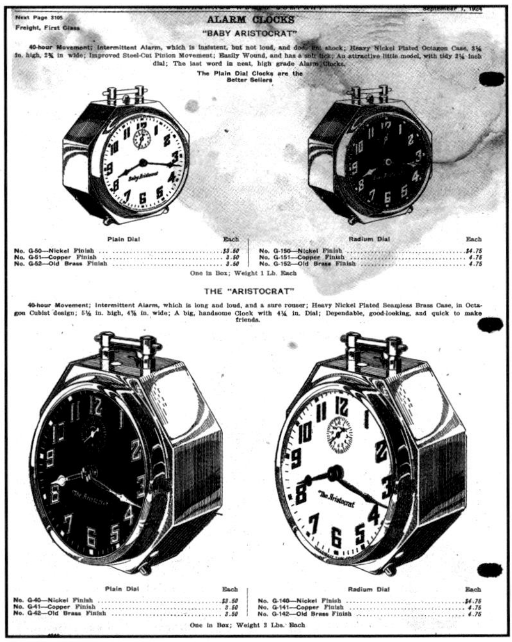

Next Page 3105 — September 1, 1924

Freight, First Class

ALARM CLOCKS

"BABY ARISTOCRAT"

40-hour Movement; Intermittent Alarm, which is insistent, but not loud, and does not shock; Heavy Nickel Plated Octagon Case, 3⅛ in. high, 2⅞ in wide; Improved Steel-Cut Pinion Movement; Easily Wound, and has a soft tick; An attractive little model, with tidy 2¼ inch dial; The last word in neat, high grade Alarm Clocks.

The Plain Dial Clocks are the Better Sellers

Plain Dial	Each	Radium Dial	Each
No. G-50—Nickel Finish	$3.50	No. G-150—Nickel Finish	$4.75
No. G-51—Copper Finish	3.50	No. G-151—Copper Finish	4.75
No. G-52—Old Brass Finish	3.50	No. G-152—Old Brass Finish	4.75

One in Box; Weight 1 Lb. Each

THE "ARISTOCRAT"

40-hour Movement; Intermittent Alarm, which is long and loud, and a sure rouser; Heavy Nickel Plated Seamless Brass Case, in Octagon Cubist design; 5⅛ in. high, 4⅞ in. wide; A big, handsome Clock with 4¼ in. Dial; Dependable, good-looking, and quick to make friends.

Plain Dial	Each	Radium Dial	Each
No. G-40—Nickel Finish	$3.50	No. G-140—Nickel Finish	$4.75
No. G-41—Copper Finish	3.50	No. G-141—Copper Finish	4.75
No. G-42—Old Brass Finish	3.50	No. G-142—Old Brass Finish	4.75

One in Box; Weight 2 Lbs. Each

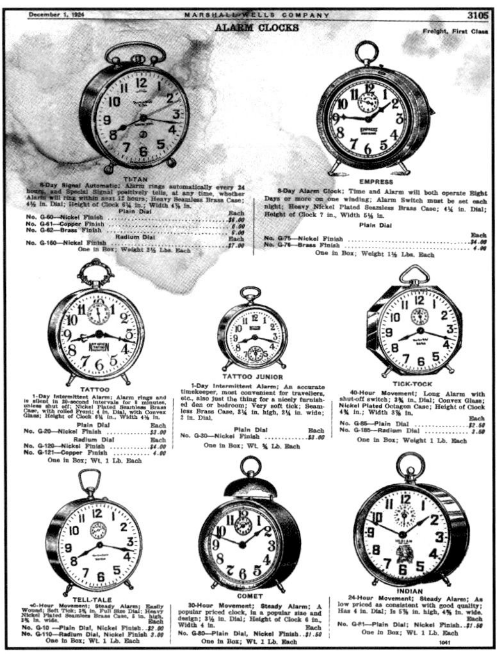

December 1, 1924 — MARSHALL-WELLS COMPANY — 3105

ALARM CLOCKS

Freight, First Class

TI-TAN

8-Day Signal Automatic; Alarm rings automatically every 24 hours, and Special Signal positively tells, at any time, whether Alarm will ring within next 12 hours; Heavy Seamless Brass Case; 4½ in. Dial; Height of Clock 6¼ in.; Width 4⅞ in.

Plain Dial	Each
No. G-60—Nickel Finish	$6.00
No. G-61—Copper Finish	6.00
No. G-62—Brass Finish	6.00
Radium Dial	**Each**
No. G-160—Nickel Finish	$7.00

One in Box; Weight 2½ Lbs. Each

EMPRESS

8-Day Alarm Clock; Time and Alarm will both operate Eight Days or more on one winding; Alarm Switch must be set each night; Heavy Nickel Plated Seamless Brass Case; 4¼ in. Dial; Height of Clock 7 in., Width 5½ in.

Plain Dial	Each
No. G-75—Nickel Finish	$4.00
No. G-76—Brass Finish	4.00

One in Box; Weight 1½ Lbs. Each

TATTOO

1-Day Intermittent Alarm; Alarm rings and is silent in 20-second intervals for 8 minutes, unless shut off; Nickel Plated Seamless Brass Case, with rolled Front; 4 in. Dial, with Convex Glass; Height of Clock 6¼ in., Width 4⅛ in.

Plain Dial	Each
No. G-20—Nickel Finish	$3.00
Radium Dial	**Each**
No. G-120—Nickel Finish	$4.00
No. G-121—Copper Finish	4.00

One in Box; Wt. 1 Lb. Each

TATTOO JUNIOR

1-Day Intermittent Alarm; An accurate timekeeper, most convenient for travellers, etc., also just the thing for a nicely furnished den or bedroom; Very soft tick; Seamless Brass Case, 3¼ in. high, 2¼ in. wide; 2 in. Dial.

Plain Dial	Each
No. G-30—Nickel Finish	$3.00

One in Box; Wt. ¾ Lb. Each

TICK-TOCK

40-Hour Movement; Long Alarm with shut-off switch; 3⅜ in. Dial; Convex Glass; Nickel Plated Octagon Case; Height of Clock 4⅝ in.; Width 3⅝ in.

	Each
No. G-85—Plain Dial	$2.50
No. G-185—Radium Dial	3.50

One in Box; Weight 1 Lb. Each

TELL-TALE

40-Hour Movement; Steady Alarm; Easily Wound; Soft Tick; 3⅝ in. Full Size Dial; Heavy Nickel Plated Seamless Brass Case, 5 in. high, 3⅝ in. wide.

	Each
No. G-10—Plain Dial, Nickel Finish	$2.00
No. G-110—Radium Dial, Nickel Finish	3.00

One in Box; Wt. 1 Lb. Each

COMET

30-Hour Movement; Steady Alarm; A popular priced clock, in a popular size and design; 3½ in. Dial; Height of Clock 6 in., Width 4 in.

	Each
No. G-80—Plain Dial, Nickel Finish	$1.50

One in Box; Wt. 1 Lb. Each

INDIAN

24-Hour Movement; Steady Alarm; As low priced as consistent with good quality; Has 4 in. Dial; Is 5⅞ in. high, 4⅝ in. wide.

	Each
No. G-81—Plain Dial; Nickel Finish	$1.50

One in Box; Wt. 1 Lb. Each

1041

The Alarm Clock with Brains

SIMPLEX
Five Inches Wide
RADIUM DIAL OR PLAIN

MANUFACTURED BY
THE ANSONIA CLOCK CO.
Makers of Fine Clocks
for Half a Century

SIMPLEX
8 DAY
Automatic Time and Alarm

Wind it but once a week

Automatically rings alarm; stops ringing and resets to ring again same time next day without further attention

Your dealer will be glad to supply you

Watchmakers! Save 1/3 to 1/2 on Tools and Materials

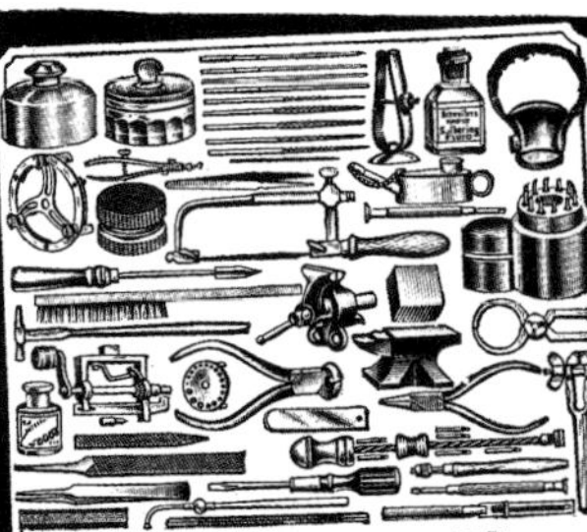

Watchmakers' Tool Set

48 Pieces in All for $14.65

Set consists of 48 pieces, including all tools necessary for watch repairing, jewelry and clock repairing. **We Pay the Postage.**

4A26—Complete set with text book.......... **$14.65** Postpaid

WE PAY THE POSTAGE ON ORDERS OF $2.00 OR MORE. UNLESS OTHERWISE STATED THE SHIPPING WEIGHT OF ANY ARTICLE ON THIS PAGE IS 3 OZ.

Send Your Order to Our Chicago Store.

If you wish to order balance staffs, jewels, mainsprings, hairsprings, etc., send a sample to us and state the name of the watch.

Old gold will be accepted by us at the market price in exchange for any article in our jewelry department. We allow 72c for 18-karat, 56c for 14-karat, 40c for 10-karat, per penny weight. We hold gold until advised that our estimate of value is satisfactory. WE MAINTAIN A WATCH REPAIR DEPARTMENT.

Lowest prices for expert workmanship. All work guaranteed. Print your name and address plainly on a tag and attach to watch. Pack the watch carefully in a substantial box and address the package to us, sending by insured mail. An estimate will be sent you immediately, before the work is begun. About two weeks are required, after we receive your answer to properly complete the work.

Genuine G. Boley Lathe

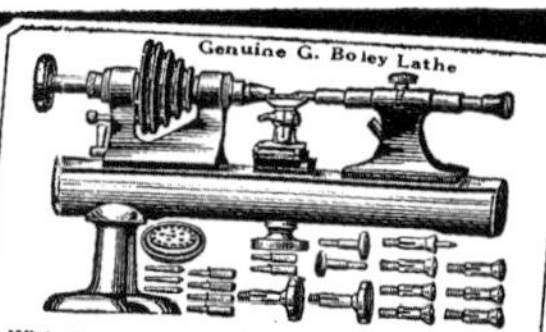

With tip over hand rests, 10 wire chucks, 10 brasses on wooden stand with glass cover, and 9 feet of belt.
4A56—We Pay Postage.............. **$42.80**

Imported lathe, similar to above, 14 wire chucks, 5 brasses and 9 feet of belt. Chucks will interchange with Webster-Whitcomb.
4A58—We Pay Postage........ **$28.75**

Watchmakers' Lathe Motor

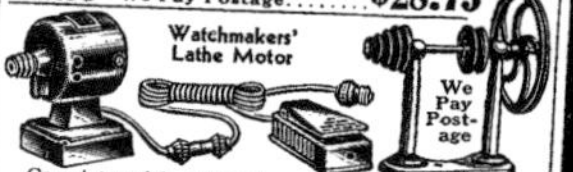

We Pay Postage

Complete with rheostat and foot device. 1/20 Horse-power. Will run forward and backward. Operated on 115 volts direct or alternating current. Rheostat regulates the speed. Height, 5½ in., length, 4¼ in. and diameter 3¼ in.
4A122—Postpaid... **$17.25**

Counter Shaft, nickel plated, wod pulley, with metal speed wheel.
4A192 **$3.25**

Send your order to our Chicago store

Watch Crystals. Thick for open face. Shpg. wt., 4 oz.
4A62
Per gross. **$4.89**
Per dozen. **.49**
Hunting style.
4A60
Per gross. **$6.49** Per dozen. **60c**

Hands, steel, for watches, hour and minute. For all watches. Not less than lots of one dozen sold. Shpg. wt., 2 oz.
4A64—Dozen pairs..... **42c**

Hands for clocks, all lengths.
4A66—Dozen pairs..... **34c**

Hands, steel, second, for all watches. Not less than 1 doz. sold. Shpg. wt., 2 oz.
4A68—Doz............ **20c**

Pendant Sleeve Driver, with nine prongs. Fits all sizes and styles of pendant sleeves.
4A118....... **90c**

Files. Needle. Length of file complete, 4 inches.
4A100—Set of 6....... **78c**

Jewelers' Files, half round or flat. Cut No. 3 or medium. **State length.**
4A142—3 inches long..... **32c**
4 inches long............... **36c**
5 inches long............... **46c**

Files. Screw Head. For filing slots in screw heads. Length, 3½ in.
4A144—Shpg. wt., 2 oz. **32c**

Pivot Files. Conical pivots for balance staffs or square for pinions. **State choice.** Length, 2 in.
4A146—Shpg. wt., 2 oz. **32c**

Roller Jewels or Ruby Pins for Elgin, Waltham, Hampden or New York Standard. All sizes. Not less than lots of 1 dozen sold. Shpg. wt., 2 oz.
4A70—Dozen.......... **52c**

Eyeglass. Hard rubber with coil spring; 2 to 5-inch focus.
4A132.......... **98c**

Eyeglass. Plain hard rubber without spring. 2 to 5-in. focus.
4A134.............. **42c**

Watch Brush. 3-row.
4A102.............. **38c**
Watch Brush. 4-row.
4A104.............. **42c**

Alcohol Cup Glass. Height, 2 in. Diam. 3 in. Shpg. wt., ¾ lb.
4A90... **41c**

Watch or Clock Oil. Shpg. wt., 4 oz.
4A92—Watch Oil... **22c**
4A93—Clock Oil.... **22c**

Watch Oiler. Nickel plated.
4A94—Shpg. wt., 2 oz... **15c**

Alcohol Spheric Lamp, glass bulb, nickel plated base. Height, 5½ inches.
Shpg. wt., 5 oz. 4A114....... **78c**

Alcohol Lamp glass bulb and cover 4 in. high. Shpg. wt., 6 oz.
4A116..... **38c**

Blow Pipe, with ball, 8 or 10 in. **State length.**
4A98—Shpg. wt., 2 oz... **34c**

Blow pipe, plain, 8 or 10 in. **State length.** Shpg. wt., 2 oz.
4A140 Each.... **18c**

Balance Staffs

Elgin Balance Staffs. All sizes. Not less than ¼ doz. sold. Shpg. wt., 2 oz.
4A78—Dozen....... **$1.08**

Waltham Balance Staffs. All sizes. Not less than ¼ dozen sold. Shpg. wt., 2 oz.
4A80—Dozen....... **$1.08**

Hampden, Illinois, Van Buren, New York Standard Balance Staffs. All sizes. Shpg. wt., 2 oz.
4A82—Dozen....... **$1.08**

Balance Hole Jewels, cock and foot, for Elgin, Waltham, Hampden or New York Standard, for all sizes. Not less than ¼ dozen sold.. Shpg. wt. 2 oz.
4A84 Dozen. **$1.04**

Balance Cap or End Stones for Elgin, Waltham, Hampden or New York Standard. All sizes. Not less than ¼ doz. sold. Shpg. wt., 2 oz.
4A86 Dozen.... **72c**

Eyeglass. Double lens. Very powerful, for very accurate work.
4A136.......... **98c**

Staking Tool

Complete in box 24 punches and 4 stumps. Postpaid, set.
4A52 **$6.25**
Same but 32 punches and 8 stumps.
4A50 $8.25
Same but 50 punches and 14 stumps
4A53 $18.10

Pliers

Pliers, flat Imported, 4-in.
4A106.. **40c**

Pliers, round. Imported. 4-inch.
4A108.. **40c**

Pliers

Pliers, end cutting. Imported. 4-inch.
4A110.. **69c**

Side cutting Imported. 4-inch.
4A112.. **69c**

Tweezers. Medium points, nickel plated.
4A148—Shpg. wt., 2 oz. **17c**

Tweezers with hand remover on opposite end.
4A150—Ship. wt., 2 oz. **27c**

Tweezers, hand remover. Shpg. wt., 2 oz.
4A152................ **48c**

Tweezers. Fine points, nickel plated.
4A154—Shpg. wt., 2 oz **17c**

Tweezers, hollow handle. Fine points, for hairsprings and fine work.
4A156—Shpg. wt., 2 oz. **29c**

Screwdrivers

Screwdriver, adjustable, pull off top for extra blades, four different sizes. Shpg. wt., 2 oz.
4A202—Complete................ **24c**

Metal Head Screwdriver, in small, medium or large size. **State size.**
4A200—Shpg. wt. 2 oz **14c**

Screwdrivers. Nickel plated. Shpg. wt., 4 oz
4A198 Set of 7...... **92c**

Pin Vises

Metal Pin Vise, adjustable.
4A124—Shpg. wt., 2 oz **27c**

Pin Vise. Hollow handle. Extra quality. Shpg. wt., 4 oz.
4A126 **78c**

Drill Stocks

Solid handle. Patent gear, 8 in. long, with 6 drills.
4A128—Shpg. wt., ¾ lb.................. **$1.13**

Drill Stock, patent spiral, 9½ in. long. 6 drills.
4A130—Shpg. wt., 5 oz... **47c**

Fits any key wind watch. Shpg. wt., 2 oz.
4A216—Patent key. **20c**

Hammers. Swiss. **State size.**
4A160
2 in.. **32c** | 2½ in. **37c**
2¼ in.. **32c** | 2¾ in. **37c**

Saw Frame. Extra quality. Shpg. wt., 6 oz.
4A170.............. **65c**

Saw Blades. Shpg. wt., 2 oz.
4A172 Per doz.... **16c**

Anvil with hub. Nickel plated, ⅝x1¾-in. Shpg. wt., 6 oz.
4A176.. **96c**

Adjustable roller remover. Nickel plated. Size, 2½-in.
4A162 Shpg. wt., 2 oz........ **$1.00**

Liquid Amber

Jewelers' Cement.
4A218......... **25c**

Granite Hold Fast Cement.
4A220......... **20c**

Vise, 1½-inch steel jaws, clamp vise, handy to adjust to any work bench. Shpg. wt., 2 lbs.
4A196.. **96c**

Gauge for watch mainsprings, with gauge for measuring thickness. Length, 4¼ inches.
4A178—Shpg. wt., 4 oz. **$1.22**

Roller Jewel Setter, nickel plated. Shpg. wt., 2 oz.
4A208 **23c**

Staking set, 24 punches. Shpg. wt., 5 oz.
4A188 **$1.27**

Drills, set of 48, assorted. Also drill stock. Shpg. wt., 5 oz.
4A190. **$1.42**

English Cutting Broaches. Set of 4. Shpg. wt., 2 oz.
4A138.... **32c**

Jobbing Stones assorted. All colors and sizes. Gross. Shpg. wt., 2 oz.
4A174 **92c**

One doz. assorted Clock Drills. Not less than 1 dozen sold.
4A120
Shpg. wt., 2 oz. Dozen...... **28c**

Winder, mainspring. Swiss. Length, 3½ inches. Shpg. wt., 4 oz.
4A204. **$1.00**

Oil-stone Slips, hard, three-corner or square, 3-in. **State choice.** Shpg. wt., 2 oz.
4A206................ **38c**

Screw Plate, double notched. 24 holes. Shpg. wt., 2 oz.
4A210.............. **$1.42**

Gravers. Set of four. Square. Shpg. wt., 2 oz.
4A212... **87c**

Movement Holders Adjustable

Style "A" Style "B"
Style "A" for pocket watches.
Style "B" for bracelet watches.
4A214—Style "A"....... **72c**
4A199—Style "B"....... **72c**

Poising Tool, for truing watch wheels.
4A97....... **85c**

Gold plated wire, round or square; in ½-ounce coils.

First Quality Round Wire. Sizes, 16 to 21 gauge.
4A166 Per ounce...... **87c**

Square Wire. Sizes, 18 to 22 gauge.
4A168.............. **87c**

Jeweled Truing Caliper. Nickel plated jeweled end for balance truing; other end for poising.
4A164............ **$1.60**

Jewel Chucks, adjustable. Set of eight. Shpg. wt., 1 oz.
4A194 **$2.12**

Gold solder. For hard soldering. Shpg. wt., 2 oz. Karat

Yellow Gold	Dwt.
4A10—Low...	24c
4A12— 6....	38c
4A14— 8....	48c
4A16—10....	68c
4A18—12....	77c
4A20—14....	87c
4A22—18....	96c

White or green gold. **State choice.**
4A17-10K **$0.85**
4A19-14K. **1.03**
4A21-18K. **1.22**

Hard soldering solution. Serves as anti-oxidizer, pickel, hard soldering fluid. Contents, 3 oz. Shpg. wt. ¾ lb.
4A24......... **42c**

Soldering Fluid, or anti-oxidizer. Shpg. wt., 4 oz.
4A186.......... **19c**

Soft Solder.
4A182.............. **14c**

Soldering Copper, small.
4A184—Shpg. wt., 4 oz.. **24c**

Silver Solder, for hard soldering or brazing. Shpg. wt., 2 oz.
4A180 Per oz. **$1.20**

Breguet and Flat Hairsprings

State size and strength. Shpg. wt. 2 oz.
4A28—Elgin Breguet......... **49c**
Breguet 4A30—Elgin Flat. **27c**
4A32—Waltham Breguet... **57c**
4A34—Waltham Flat....... **33c**
4A36—Hamilton Breguet... **62c**
4A38—Hampden Breguet.. **49c**
4A40—Hampden Flat............ **32c**
4A42—Illinois Breguet.......... **57c**
4A44—Ill. Flat... **27c**
4A46—N. Y. Standard Breguet................ **30c**
4A48—N. Y. Standard Flat. **26c**
Flat

Mainspring for watches. All styles and sizes. Not less than ¼ dozen sold. Shpg. wt., 3 oz.
A B C
4A72—Dozen....... **$1.36**

Mainsprings for clocks.
4A74—1-day. Shpg. wt., 2 oz... **15c**
4A76—8-day. Shpg. wt., 7 oz... **33c**
Mention width wanted.

SEND ALL ORDERS FOR WATCHMAKERS' TOOLS AND MATERIALS TO OUR CHICAGO STORE
SEARS, ROEBUCK AND CO., CHICAGO, ILL.

F8912(F4WT) 6.17.31

WINDING KEYS FOR AMERICAN CLOCKS.

Prices Per Dozen.

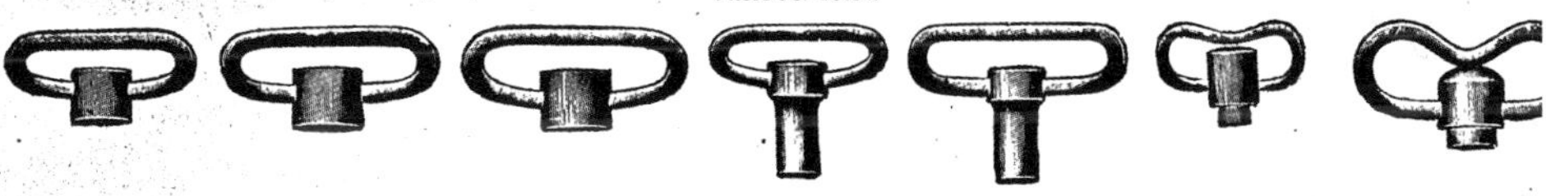

WATERBURY SUNRISE Alarm No. 22. 40c

WATERBURY SUNRISE Time No. 23. 40c

WATERBURY SUNRISE Time No. 24. 40c

WATERBURY PATROL Alarm No. 25. 40c

WATERBURY PATROL Time No. 26. 40c

INGRAHAM Alarm No. 27. 50c

INGRAHAM Time No. 28. 60c

ANSONIA SPARK 1 Day Time No. 29. 50c

ANSONIA PIRATE Time No. 30. 60c

ANSONIA PEEP O' DAY Time and Alarm No. 31. 60c

ANSONIA CLIMAX Time and Alarm No. 32. 75c

ANSONIA PRINCESS 8 Day Time No. 33. 75c

ANSONIA SPARK 8 Day Time No. 34. 75c

SETH THOMAS No. 35. 50c

SETH THOMAS No. 36. 50c

SETH THOMAS No. 37. 50c

SETH THOMAS No. 38. 50c

SETH THOMAS No. 39. 50c

SETH THOMAS No. 40. 50c

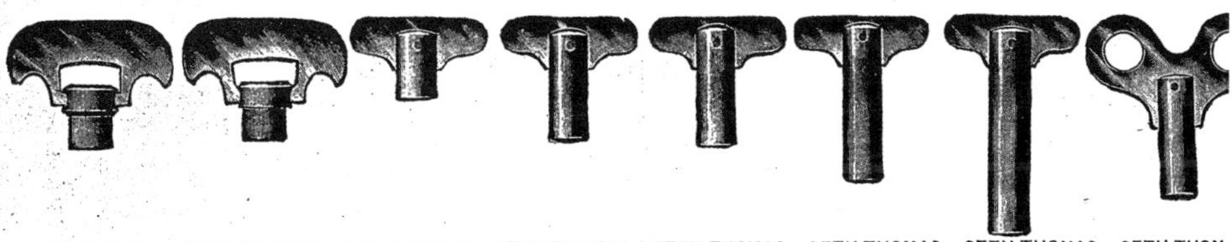

SETH THOMAS No. 41. 50c

SETH THOMAS No. 42. 50c

SETH THOMAS No. 43. 50c

SETH THOMAS No. 44. 50c

SETH THOMAS No. 45. 50c

SETH THOMAS No. 46. 50c

SETH THOMAS No. 47. 50c

SETH THOM[illegible] No. 48. 50c

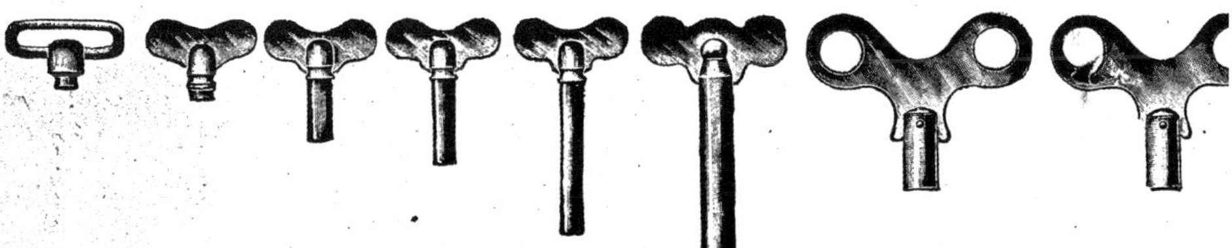

GILBERT Leatherette Time No. 49. 30c

GILBERT 2" Movement Time No. 50. 25c

GILBERT Fit-Up Time No. 51. 30c

GILBER. Autogetup Alarm No. 52. 35c

GILBERT Autogetup Time No. 53. 35c

GILBERT Best Alarm No. 54. 40c

GILBERT Terror Alarm Right Thread No. 55. 45c

GILBERT Terror Time Left Thread No. 56. 45c

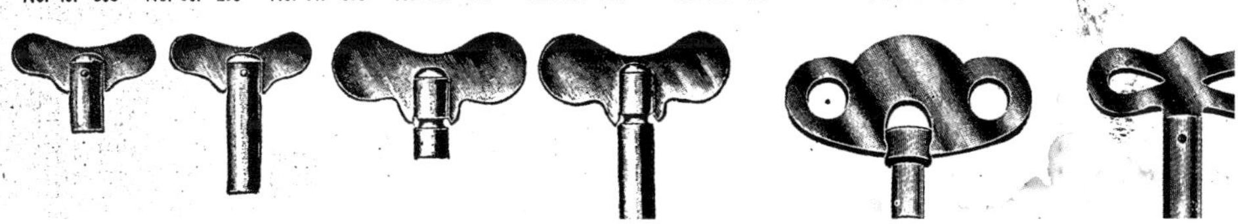

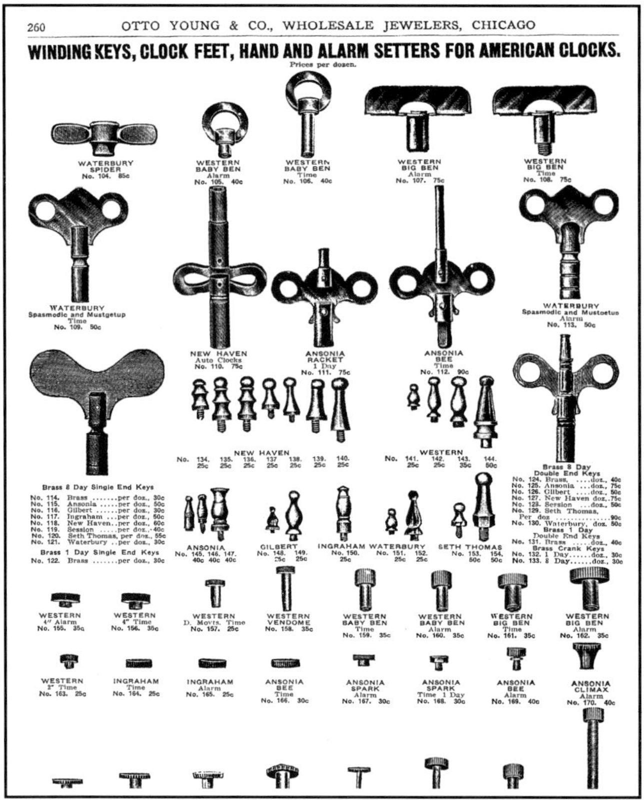

260 OTTO YOUNG & CO., WHOLESALE JEWELERS, CHICAGO

WINDING KEYS, CLOCK FEET, HAND AND ALARM SETTERS FOR AMERICAN CLOCKS.

Prices per dozen.

WATERBURY SPIDER No. 104. 85c

WESTERN BABY BEN Alarm No. 105. 40c

WESTERN BABY BEN Time No. 106. 40c

WESTERN BIG BEN Alarm No. 107. 75c

WESTERN BIG BEN Time No. 108. 75c

WATERBURY Spasmodic and Mustgetup Time No. 109. 50c

NEW HAVEN Auto Clocks No. 110. 75c

ANSONIA RACKET 1 Day No. 111. 75c

ANSONIA BEE Time No. 112. 90c

WATERBURY Spasmodic and Mustoetup Alarm No. 113. 50c

NEW HAVEN No. 134. 25c, 135. 25c, 136. 25c, 137 25c, 138. 25c, 139. 25c, 140. 25c

WESTERN No. 141. 25c, 142. 25c, 143. 35c, 144. 50c

Brass 8 Day Single End Keys

No. 114. Brass ....per doz., 30c
No. 115. Ansonia .....per doz., 50c
No. 116. Gilbert ......per doz., 30c
No. 117. Ingraham ...per doz., 50c
No. 118. New Haven..per doz., 60c
No. 119. Session .....per doz., 40c
No. 120. Seth Thomas, per doz., 55c
No. 121. Waterbury ..per doz., 30c

Brass 1 Day Single End Keys

No. 122. Brass ....per doz., 30c

ANSONIA No. 145. 40c, 146. 40c, 147. 40c

GILBERT No. 148. 25c, 149. 25c

INGRAHAM No. 150. 25c

WATERBURY No. 151. 25c, 152. 25c

SETH THOMAS No. 153. 50c, 154. 50c

Brass 8 Day Double End Keys

No. 124. Brass, ...doz., 40c
No. 125. Ansonia ...doz., 75c
No. 126. Gilbert ....doz., 50c
No. 127. New Haven doz., 75c
No. 123. Session ...doz., 50c
No. 129. Seth Thomas, Per doz 90c
No. 130. Waterbury, doz. 50c

Brass 1 Day Double End Keys

No. 131. Brass .....doz., 40c

Brass Crank Keys

No. 132. 1 Day......doz., 30c
No. 133. 8 Day......doz., 30c

WESTERN 4" Alarm No. 155. 35c

WESTERN 4" Time No. 156. 35c

WESTERN D. Movts. Time No. 157. 25c

WESTERN VENDOME No. 158. 35c

WESTERN BABY BEN Time No. 159. 35c

WESTERN BABY BEN Alarm No. 160. 35c

WESTERN BIG BEN Time No. 161. 35c

WESTERN BIG BEN Alarm No. 162. 35c

WESTERN 2" Time No. 163. 25c

INGRAHAM Time No. 164. 25c

INGRAHAM Alarm No. 165. 25c

ANSONIA BEE Time No. 166. 30c

ANSONIA SPARK Alarm No. 167. 30c

ANSONIA SPARK Time 1 Day No. 168. 30c

ANSONIA BEE Alarm No. 169. 40c

ANSONIA CLIMAX Alarm No. 170. 40c

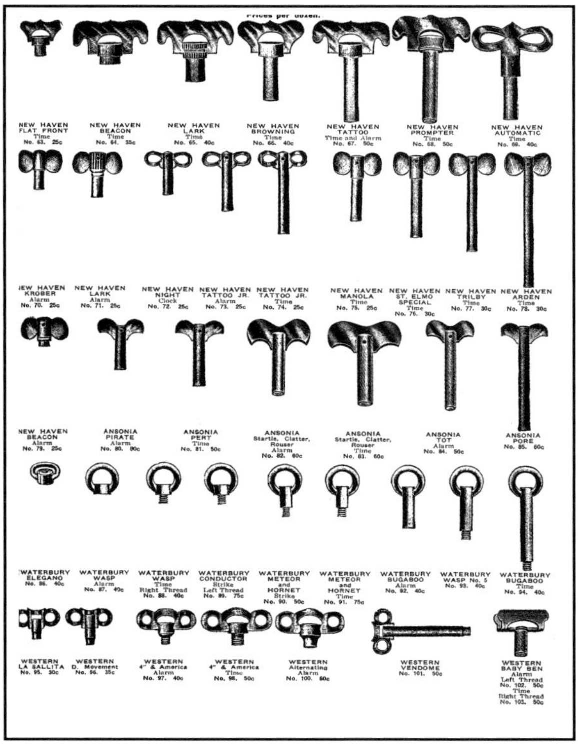

Prices per dozen.

NEW HAVEN FLAT FRONT Time No. 63. 25c

NEW HAVEN BEACON Time No. 64. 35c

NEW HAVEN LARK Time No. 65. 40c

NEW HAVEN BROWNING Time No. 66. 40c

NEW HAVEN TATTOO Time and Alarm No. 67. 50c

NEW HAVEN PROMPTER Time No. 68. 50c

NEW HAVEN AUTOMATIC Time No. 69. 40c

NEW HAVEN KROBER Alarm No. 70. 25c

NEW HAVEN LARK Alarm No. 71. 25c

NEW HAVEN NIGHT Clock No. 72. 25c

NEW HAVEN TATTOO JR. Alarm No. 73. 25c

NEW HAVEN TATTOO JR. Time No. 74. 25c

NEW HAVEN MANOLA Time No. 75. 25c

NEW HAVEN ST. ELMO SPECIAL Time No. 76. 30c

NEW HAVEN TRILBY Time No. 77. 30c

NEW HAVEN ARDEN Time No. 78. 30c

NEW HAVEN BEACON Alarm No. 79. 25c

ANSONIA PIRATE Alarm No. 80. 90c

ANSONIA PERT Time No. 81. 50c

ANSONIA Startle, Clatter, Rouser Alarm No. 82. 60c

ANSONIA Startle, Clatter, Rouser Time No. 83. 60c

ANSONIA TOT Alarm No. 84. 50c

ANSONIA PORE No. 85. 60c

WATERBURY ELEGANO No. 86. 40c

WATERBURY WASP Alarm No. 87. 40c

WATERBURY WASP Time Right Thread No. 88. 40c

WATERBURY CONDUCTOR Strike Left Thread No. 89. 75c

WATERBURY METEOR and HORNET Strike No. 90. 50c

WATERBURY METEOR and HORNET Time No. 91. 75c

WATERBURY BUGABOO Alarm No. 92. 40c

WATERBURY WASP No. 5 No. 93. 40c

WATERBURY BUGABOO Time No. 94. 40c

WESTERN LA SALLITA No. 95. 30c

WESTERN D. Movement No. 96. 35c

WESTERN 4" & America Alarm No. 97. 40c

WESTERN 4" & America Time No. 98. 50c

WESTERN Alternating Alarm No. 100. 60c

WESTERN VENDOME No. 101. 50c

WESTERN BABY BEN Alarm Left Thread No. 102. 50c Time Right Thread No. 103. 50c

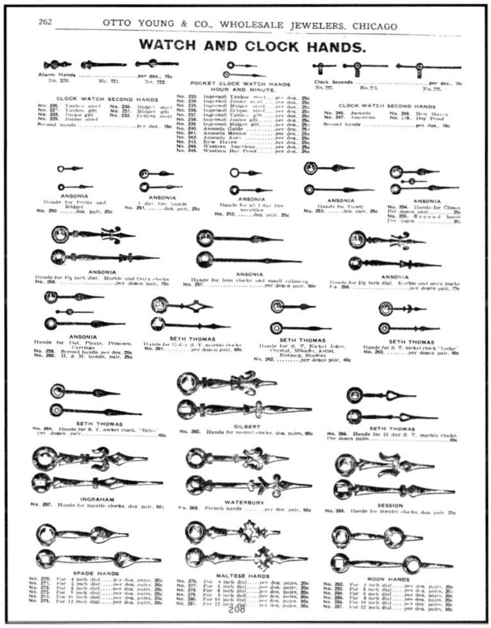
262
OTTO YOUNG & CO., WHOLESALE JEWELERS, CHICAGO
WATCH AND CLOCK HANDS.
Alarm Hands ... per doz., 15c
No. 220. No. 221. No. 222.
POCKET CLOCK WATCH HANDS HOUR AND MINUTE.
Clock Seconds ... per doz., 15c
CLOCK WATCH SECOND HANDS
CLOCK WATCH SECOND HANDS
ANSONIA
ANSONIA
ANSONIA
ANSONIA
ANSONIA
ANSONIA
ANSONIA
ANSONIA
ANSONIA
SETH THOMAS
SETH THOMAS
SETH THOMAS
SETH THOMAS
GILBERT
SETH THOMAS
INGRAHAM
WATERBURY
SESSION
SPADE HANDS
MALTESE HANDS
MOON HANDS
208

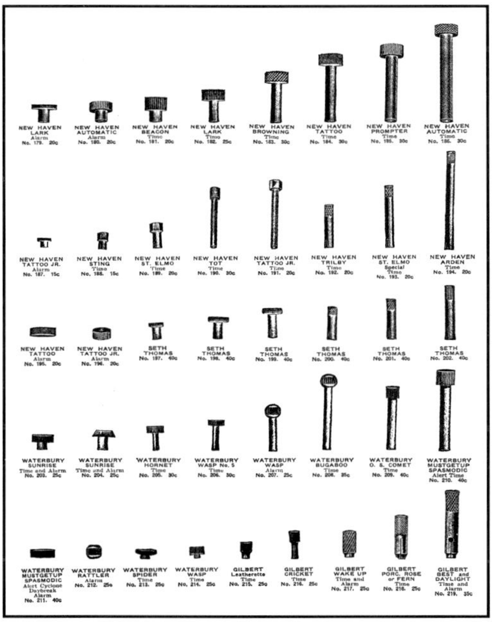
NEW HAVEN LARK Alarm No. 179. 20c
NEW HAVEN AUTOMATIC Alarm No. 180. 20c
NEW HAVEN BEACON Time No. 181. 20c
NEW HAVEN LARK Time No. 182. 25c
NEW HAVEN BROWNING Time No. 183. 30c
NEW HAVEN TATTOO Time No. 184. 30c
NEW HAVEN PROMPTER Time No. 185. 30c
NEW HAVEN AUTOMATIC Time No. 186. 30c
NEW HAVEN TATTOO JR. Alarm No. 187. 15c
NEW HAVEN STING Time No. 188. 15c
NEW HAVEN ST. ELMO Time No. 189. 20c
NEW HAVEN TOT Time No. 190. 30c
NEW HAVEN TATTOO JR. Time No. 191. 20c
NEW HAVEN TRILBY Time No. 192. 20c
NEW HAVEN ST. ELMO Special Time No. 193. 20c
NEW HAVEN ARDEN Time No. 194. 20c
NEW HAVEN TATTOO Alarm No. 195. 20c
NEW HAVEN TATTOO JR. Alarm No. 196. 20c
SETH THOMAS No. 197. 40c
SETH THOMAS No. 198. 40c
SETH THOMAS No. 199. 40c
SETH THOMAS No. 200. 40c
SETH THOMAS No. 201. 40c
SETH THOMAS No. 202. 40c
WATERBURY SUNRISE Time and Alarm No. 203. 25c
WATERBURY SUNRISE Time and Alarm No. 204. 25c
WATERBURY HORNET Time No. 205. 30c
WATERBURY WASP No. 5 Time No. 206. 30c
WATERBURY WASP Alarm No. 207. 25c
WATERBURY BUGABOO Time No. 208. 35c
WATERBURY O. S. COMET Time No. 209. 40c
WATERBURY MUSTGETUP SPASMODIC Alert Time No. 210. 40c
WATERBURY MUSTGETUP SPASMODIC Alert Cyclone Daybreak Alarm No. 211. 40c
WATERBURY RATTLER Alarm No. 212. 25c
WATERBURY SPIDER Time No. 213. 25c
WATERBURY WASP Time No. 214. 25c
GILBERT Leatherette Time No. 215. 25c
GILBERT CRICKET Time No. 216. 25c
GILBERT WAKE UP Time and Alarm No. 217. 25c
GILBERT PORC. ROSE or FERN Time No. 218. 25c
GILBERT BEST and DAYLIGHT Time and Alarm No. 219. 35c

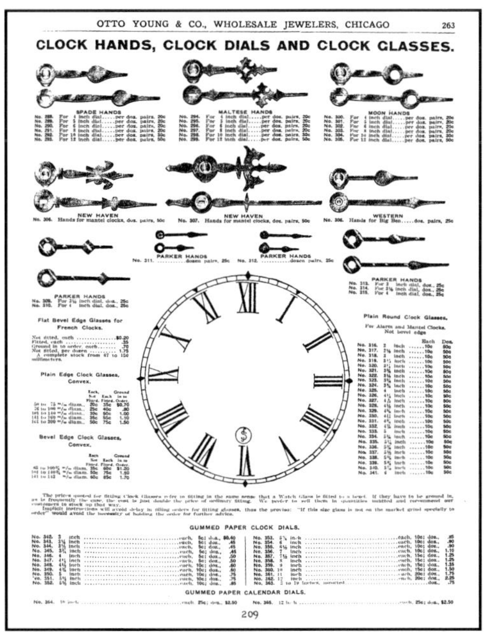
OTTO YOUNG & CO., WHOLESALE JEWELERS, CHICAGO
263
CLOCK HANDS, CLOCK DIALS AND CLOCK GLASSES.
SPADE HANDS
MALTESE HANDS
MOON HANDS
NEW HAVEN
NEW HAVEN
WESTERN
PARKER HANDS
PARKER HANDS
PARKER HANDS
PARKER HANDS
Flat Bevel Edge Glasses for French Clocks.
Plain Edge Clock Glasses, Convex.
Bevel Edge Clock Glasses, Convex.
Plain Round Clock Glasses.
GUMMED PAPER CLOCK DIALS.
GUMMED PAPER CALENDAR DIALS.
209

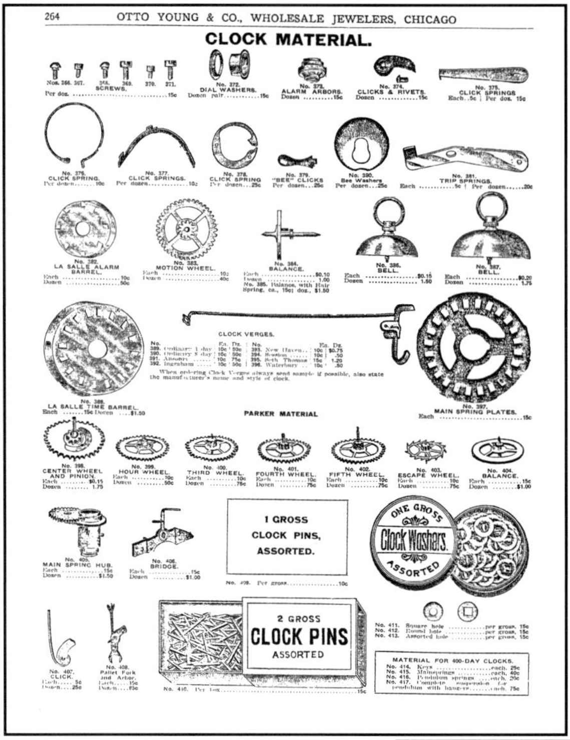

264 OTTO YOUNG & CO., WHOLESALE JEWELERS, CHICAGO

CLOCK MATERIAL.

Nos. 366. 367. 368. 369. 370. 371. SCREWS. Per doz. 15c

No. 372. DIAL WASHERS. Dozen pair....15c

No. 373. ALARM ARBORS. Dozen 15c

No. 374. CLICKS & RIVETS. Dozen 15c

No. 375. CLICK SPRINGS. Each..5c | Per doz. 15c

No. 376. CLICK SPRING. Per dozen....10c

No. 377. CLICK SPRINGS. Per dozen....10c

No. 378. CLICK SPRING Per dozen...25c

No. 379. "BEE" CLICKS Per dozen...25c

No. 380. Bee Washers Per dozen...25c

No. 381. TRIP SPRINGS. Each ....5c | Per dozen....20c

No. 382. LA SALLE ALARM BARREL. Each ....10c Dozen 50c

No. 383. MOTION WHEEL. Each ....10c Dozen 40c

No. 384. BALANCE. Each ....$0.10 Dozen ....1.00 No. 385. Balance, with Hair Spring, ea., 15c; doz., $1.50

No. 386. BELL. Each ....$0.15 Dozen 1.50

No. 387. BELL. Each ....$0.20 Dozen 1.75

CLOCK VERGES.

No.		Ea.	Dz.	No.		Ea.	Dz.
389.	Ordinary 1 day	10c	50c	393.	New Haven..	10c	$0.75
390.	Ordinary 8 day	10c	50c	394.	Session	10c	.50
391.	Ansonia	10c	75c	395.	Seth Thomas	15c	1.20
392.	Ingraham	10c	50c	396.	Waterbury ..	10c	.50

When ordering Clock Verges always send sample if possible, also state the manufacturer's name and style of clock.

No. 388. LA SALLE TIME BARREL. Each ....15c Dozen $1.50

No. 397. MAIN SPRING PLATES. Each 15c

PARKER MATERIAL

No. 398. CENTER WHEEL AND PINION. Each ....$0.15 Dozen 1.75

No. 399. HOUR WHEEL. Each ....10c Dozen 50c

No. 400. THIRD WHEEL. Each ....10c Dozen 75c

No. 401. FOURTH WHEEL. Each ....10c Dozen 75c

No. 402. FIFTH WHEEL. Each ....10c Dozen 75c

No. 403. ESCAPE WHEEL. Each ....10c Dozen 75c

No. 404. BALANCE. Each ....15c Dozen $1.00

No. 405. MAIN SPRING HUB. Each ....15c Dozen $1.50

No. 406. BRIDGE. Each ....15c Dozen $1.00

1 GROSS CLOCK PINS, ASSORTED.

No. 409. Per gross....10c

ONE GROSS Clock Washers. ASSORTED

No. 407. CLICK. Each.... 5c Dozen....25c

No. 408. Pallet Fork and Arbor. Each....15c Dozen....85c

2 GROSS CLOCK PINS ASSORTED

No. 410. Per box....15c

No. 411. Square hole ....per gross, 15c
No. 412. Round hole ....per gross, 15c
No. 413. Assorted hole ....per gross, 15c

MATERIAL FOR 400-DAY CLOCKS.
No. 414. Keys ....each, 25c
No. 415. Mainsprings ....each, 40c
No. 416. Pendulum springs ....each, 20c
No. 417. Complete suspension for pendulum with hangers....each, 75c

OTTO YOUNG & CO., WHOLESALE JEWELERS, CHICAGO 267

AMERICAN CLOCK SPRINGS.

No.		Wid'h Inch	Style of End	Price Each	Price Dozen
	ANSCNIA.				
484	1-day Spark, Time	¼	Loop	$0.10	$0.75
485	1-day Spark, Alarm	¼	Hole	.10	.75
486	Startle, Alarm	⅜	Loop	.15	1.25
487	1-day Midge	¼	Loop	.10	.75
488	Jigger	¼	Loop	.10	.75
489	8-day Midge	11/32	Hole	.15	1.75
490	8-day Spark	⅝	Hole	.25	2.50
491	Round V. E., Time	¾	Hole	.25	2.75
492	Gresham, Time	¾	Loop	.25	2.50
493	8-day Marine, Time	13/32	Loop	.25	2.75
494	Bee, Time	¼	Hole	.15	1.50
495	Peep O-Day, Time	⅜	Hole	.15	1.25
496	New Marine, Time	⅝	Hole	.15	1.75
497	Pirate, Alarm	¼	Loop	.10	.75
498	Long Alarm, Alarm	7/16	Loop	.15	1.50
499	Novelty and Spark	¼	Loop	.10	.75
500	Tally Ho, Strike	½	Hole	.15	1.75
501	Dot, Strike	7/16	Loop	.15	1.50
502	30-hour Strike	⅝	Loop	.10	1.00
503	Pirate, Repeater, etc., Time	⅜	Loop	.10	1.00
504	Square V. E., Strike	¾	Loop	.25	2.50
505	Diamond and Small, 8-day	¾	Loop	.25	2.50
506	Regulator, Time	⅝	Loop	.20	2.00
507	Duplex	9/16	Loop	.15	1.80
508	Dot, Time	7/16	Loop	.15	1.25
509	Round V. E., Strike	¾	Hole	.25	2.75
	NEW HAVEN.				
510	Auto, Alarm	¼	Loop	.10	.75
511	Beacon, Alarm	¼	Loop	.10	.75
512	Champion, Alarm	¼	Loop	.10	.75
513	Mauser, Alarm	¼	Loop	.10	.75
514	Sprite, Alarm	¼	Loop	.10	.75
515	Tattoo, Alarm	⅜	Loop	.10	.75
516	Tattoo, Jr., Alarm	7/32	Loop	.10	.75
517	Mauser, Alarm	7/32	Loop	.10	.75
518	Beacon, Alarm	7/32	Loop	.10	.75
519	St. Elmo, N. M.	7/32	Loop	.10	.75
520	Germ, Time (Alarm not made)	7/32	Loop	.10	.75
521	Sting, Time	7/32	Loop	.10	.75
522	Sting, Time (Alarm not made)	5/16	Loop	.10	.75
523	St. Elmo, Time, O. M.	5/16	Loop	.10	.75
524	Tattoo, Time	⅜	Loop	.10	.75
525	Mauser & Beacon, Time	⅜	Loop	.10	.75
526	Sprite, Time	⅜	Loop	.10	.75
527	Auto, Time	⅜	Loop	.10	.75
528	Champion, Time	⅜	Loop	.10	.75
529	Tattoo, Jr., Time	9/32	Loop	.10	.75
530	St. Elmo, 8-day	7/16	Loop	.10	1.00
531	Sting, 8-day	7/16	Loop	.10	1.00
532	Victory, Time and Alarm	½	Loop	.15	1.50
533	Small, 8-day Duplex	½	Loop	.20	2.00
534	Lubec Movt., Time	½	Loop	.15	1.50
535	Lubec Movt., Strike	½	Loop	.15	1.50
536	Small and Large, 8-day Strike	⅝	Loop	.20	2.40
537	No. 43 Time Spring	⅝	Loop	.20	2.00
538	No. 43 Strike Spring	½	Loop	.20	2.00
539	Round Columbus, Time	5/16	Loop	.15	1.25
540	Round Columbus, Strike	5/16	Loop	.15	1.25
541	Combs Movts., Time	¾	Loop	.25	2.50
542	Blackwood Movts., Time and Strike	¾	Loop	.25	2.50
543	Large, 8-day Time & 8-day T. P. Spg.	¾	Loop	.25	2.50
544	Japan Lever, T. P. Time	⅝	Hole	.20	2.00
	SETH THOMAS.				
545	For 2-inch Dial Clock	5/16	Loop	.10	.75
546	½-inch, 8-day	½	Loop	.20	2.00
547	¾-inch, 8-day	¾	Loop	.25	2.50
548	8-day, for Barrel	¾	Hole	.25	2.50
549	Novelty Clock	¼	Loop	.10	.75
550	Colt	5/16	Hole	.10	1.00
551	Echo, Alarm	3/16	Loop	.10	.75
552	Joker, Alarm	¼	Loop	.10	.75
553	Dix, Alarm	7/16	Loop	.10	1.00
554	Dix, Time	⅜	Loop	.10	.75
555	Long, Alarm	½	Loop	.20	2.00
556	Echo, Time	3/16	Loop	.10	.75
	GILBERT.				
557	No. I 110, Time	11/32	Hole	$0.15	$1.25
558	Alarm Spring	¼	Loop	.10	.75
559	Wake-Up, Alarm	¼	Loop	.10	.75
560	Hello, Alarm	11/32	Loop	.10	1.00
561	Wake-Up, Time	5/16	Loop	.15	1.25
562	Surprise Spring	11/32	Loop	.15	1.25
563	No. 30, Strike	5/16	Loop	.20	2.00
564	No. I 110, Alarm	⅛	Loop	.10	1.00
565	No. 27, Time	⅜	Loop	.15	1.50
566	O. S., 30-hour Movt	9/32	Loop	.20	2.00
567	No. 32, Time	13/32	Hole	.20	2.00
568	No. 32, Strike	5/16	Hole	.20	2.00
569	Blackwood's Time and Strike	¾	Loop	.25	2.50
570	8-day Spring for No. I 210	⅝	Hole	.15	1.50
	INGRAHAM.				
571	Ratler, Alarm	¼	Loop	.10	.60
572	Ratler, Autocrat, Rotator, Time	⅜	Loop	.15	1.25
573	Autocrat, Rotator, Alarm	11/32	Loop	.10	1.00
574	8-day, Time	¾	Loop	.25	2.50
	PARKER.				
575	For all numbers, Time	⅜	Loop	.15	1.25
576	For No. 60 and 61, Time	5/16	Hole	.10	1.00
577	For No. 60 and 61, Alarm	¼	Hole	.10	.75
578	For No. 100, 102, 103, 104, 105, 106, Alarm	⅜	Loop	.10	.75
579	For No. 97 and 98, Alarm	⅜	Loop	.10	1.00
580	PRINCETON	11/32	Hole	.10	.75
581	PLATO	11/32	Hole	.10	.75
	SESSION.				
582	1-day Marine	5/16	Hole	.10	1.00
583	Verdi, Time and No. 3 Regulator	⅝	Loop	.20	2.00
584	8-day Marine	⅝	Hole	.20	2.00
585	Verdi, Strike and Hall Clocks	11/16	Loop	.20	2.40
586	8-day Parlor and Kitchen	¾	Loop	.25	2.50
	WATERBURY.				
587	Wasp, Bugaboo, Time	5/16	Hole	.10	.60
588	Wasp, Alarm	3/16	Loop	.10	.60
589	Sunrise, Caliph, Alarm	7/32	Loop	.10	.60
590	Sunrise, Time	⅜	Hole	.10	.75
591	Mustgetup, Spasmodic, Alarm	½	Loop	.15	1.50
592	Mustgetup, Spasmodic, Time	⅜	Loop	.10	.75
593	Automobile, Mainspring	⅝	Hole	.20	2.00
594	Cavalier, etc., Mainspring	¾	Hole	.25	2.50
595	All 1-day 6-in. and 8-in. Lever, Strike	⅝	Hole	.25	2.50
596	Seine, etc., Strike and Time	7/16	Hole	.25	2.50
597	Judson, Java, Strike and Time	¾	Loop	.25	2.75
598	Ship's Bell, Strike	¾	Hole	.25	2.50
599	Ship's Bell, Time	⅝	Hole	.25	2.50
600	Special, Time	½	Loop	.20	2.00
601	Fan G, Spider, Comet, Time	¾	Hole	.25	2.50
602	All 8-in. and 12-in. Lever, Strike	¾	Loop	.25	2.50
603	Guide, Alarm	¼	Hole	.10	.60
604	Comet, Strike	5/16	Hole	.10	.60
605	All 1-day, 6-inch and 8-inch Levers, Strike	5/16	Loop	.10	.75
606	All 8-day, 6-inch, 8-inch and 12-inch Levers, Time	1	Hole	.30	3.50
607	Nabob, Viceroy, Time	11/16	Hole	.20	2.00
608	Florida and Motorboat, Time	¾	Hole	.25	2.50
609	Guide, Strike	⅜	Loop	10	.75
610	Daybreak, Alarm	5/16	Loop	.10	.60
	WESTERN.				
611	4-inch Dial, Time	5/16	Hole	.10	.75
612	2-inch Dial, Time	7/32	Loop	.10	.75
613	America, Alarm	3/16	Hole	.10	.60
614	Ironclad, Alarm	3/16	Hole	.10	.60
615	Strenuous and Alternating Alarm	5/16	Loop	.10	.75
616	Big Ben, Alarm	½	Loop	.10	1.00
617	Baby Ben, Time	¼	Hole	.10	.75
618	Baby Ben, Alarm	7/32	Hole	.10	.75

211

Two printers blocks, Big Ben and Gilbert.

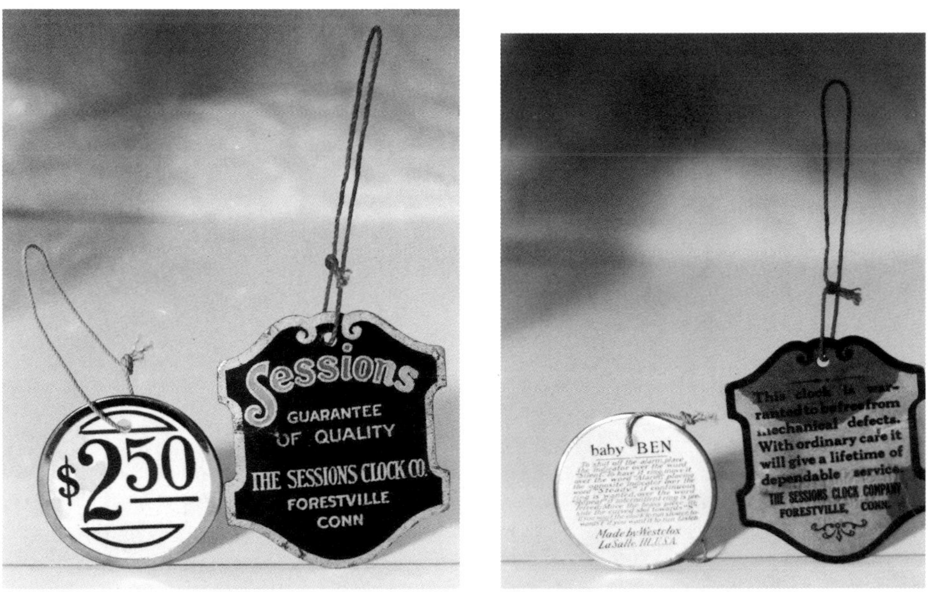

Two advertising tags, Baby Ben and Sessions.

Private Label Clocks

A retailer could order a case of clocks and have his business advertised on the dial at no additional charge. I am sure I have barely scratched the surface, but I have listed the businesses I know. Information includes advertising as it appears on the dial, what type of clock it is on, and either a manufacturer's date or a patent date.

California

Garrett Owen
Jeweler and Silversmith
So. Berkley, Cal
Parker

Illinois

Emerick & Barrett
Jewelers & Opticians
Freeport, Ills.
Patented Jan. 29-1901
10-31-1912 scratched on back
Waterbury

Iowa

W.W. Hazelton
Jeweler
Calmar, Iowa
Mfg'd 11-12-1914
Big Ben

Edwin Pape
Jeweler
Davenport, Iowa
Patented Jan. 25-1898
12-27-02 scratched on back
Patented Dec. 23-1903
Gilbert
Parker

W.G. Leslie & Co.
Eldora, Iowa
Mfg'd 10-19-1912
Big Ben

C.R. Runkle
Jeweler
Lisbon, Iowa
Patented Nov. 29-1910
Waterbury

D.L. Hoefle
Jeweler
Newell, Iowa
Mfg'd 10-29-1914
Big Ben

F.D. Gibbs
Jeweler
Sanborn, Iowa
Mfg'd 9-6-1924
Big Ben

Massachusetts

Andrews Jewelers
276 Washington St.
Cor. Water St.
Boston
Mfg'd 8-12-1914
Eska Mfg.
(Westclox)

Minnesota

W.M. James
Jeweler
Breckenridge, Minn.
2 known
Mfg'd 10-13-1913
3-18-1915
Big Ben

John Dwyer
Jeweler
Chisholm, Minn.
Mfg'd 5-20-1915
Big Ben

C.D. Leidal
Jeweler and Optician
Fergus Fall, Minn.
Mfg'd 7-9-1918
Big Ben

F.H. Straub
Optometrist and Jeweler
Fergus Falls, Minn.
Mfg'd 10-15-1926
Big Ben

B. Gerber
Jeweler and Optician
Frazee, Minn.
Mfg'd 10-21-1915
Big Ben

Lilieberg Bros.
Jewelers
123 North 3rd St.
Minneapolis, Minn.
Mfg'd 6-19-1917
Big Ben

O.H. Olson
Jeweler
Paynesville, Minn.
Mfg'd 10-22-1914
Big Ben

Edwin P. Long
Jeweler
St. Cloud, Minn.
Patented Jan. 29-1901
Waterbury

Nebraska

Spork & Darling
Jewelers
Hartington, Neb.
Big Ben

New York

Autodraft Mfg. Co.
New York City
Patented June 7-1921
Waterbury

North Dakota

P.E. Johnson
Jeweler and Optician
Abercrombie, N.D.
Mfg'd 3-14-1914
Big Ben

Carl W. Slocum
Jeweler
Cando, N.D.
Mfg'd 5-17-1918
Big Ben

R.E. Kreader
Jeweler
Cogswell, N.D.
Mfg'd 2-10-1914
Big Ben

Hagen-Newton
Jewelers
Fargo, N.D.
10-10-19 scratched on back
Big Ben

Walter R. Blakely
Jeweler and Optician
Grafton, N.D.
Mfg'd 9-14-1912
Big Ben

A.G. Foogman
Jeweler & Optician
Hillsboro, N.D.
Mfg'd 1-18-1921
Big Ben

A.G. Tellner
Jeweler and Optician
Jamestown, N.D.
Mfg'd 3-13-1916
Baby Ben

M.A. Worcester & Co.
Lidgerwood, N.D.
Mfg'd 1-21-1909
Westclox
Alternating

Chas. A. Frost
Jeweler
Lisbon, N.D.
Mfg'd 1-31-1918
Big Ben

C. Lund
New Rockford, N.D.
Patented Jan. 29-1907
Waterbury

Oriska Hdwe. Impl't Co.
Oriska, N.D.
Patented Nov. 20-1890
New Haven

W.W. Thompson
Jeweler
Park River, N.D.
Mfg'd 12-6-1918
Big Ben

Lloyd A. Morrison
Jeweler
Valley City, N.D.
Mfg'd 8-8-1914
Big Ben

Nerseth & Fauchald
White Earth, N.D.
Patented Nov. 29-1898
New Haven

Ohio

W.H. Broer
427 Summit St.
Toledo, Ohio
Patented Jan. 19-1909
Gilbert

South Dakota

W.N. Matthews
Alexandria, S.D.
Mfg'd 2-26-1926
Big Ben

Washington

Edwin Milberg
Watchmaker, Jeweler, Engraver
Colville, Wash.
Mfg'd 10-16-1913
Big Ben

Stone-Fisher Co.
Tacoma, Wash.
Mfg'd 8-7-1919
Big Ben

Wisconsin

J.W. Wightman
Elroy, Wisc.
Mfg'd 4-25-1914
Big Ben